# Advance praise for *The Secret Life of the Dyslexic Child*:

"A sage Sioux proverb reminds us to 'never judge a man until you have walked a mile in his moccasins.' **Dr. Robert Frank's brilliant new book**, *The Secret Life of the Dyslexic Child*, provides parents and professionals with a **unique opportunity to experience the world through the eyes and ears of a person with dyslexia.** His blazing insights enable the reader—perhaps for the first time—to truly understand the struggles of the dyslexic learner.

The term *dyslexia* has been part of the American lexicon for decades, but the disorder continues to be greatly misunderstood. 'Dyslexia' has become the punch line for innumerable tasteless and obvious jokes; it has also come to be viewed in some quarters as "a gift" that features creativity, brilliance, and perception. Dr. Frank provides a great service by guiding the reader to **a realistic, sensitive understanding of the true nature of dyslexia**—a puzzling, frustrating, pervasive disorder that can significantly compromise and complicate a person's life. However, he also provides dozens of **strategies that can be used to maximize the dyslexic person's potential** and promote true and lasting progress.

Dr. Frank's book provides the reader with information and inspiration to more effectively deal with the challenge of dyslexia. The readable format of the book features innumerable sidebars and anecdotes that the reader will use again and again. This volume marks **a significant contribution to the field**—and an invaluable opportunity to gain insight into our fellow travelers who struggle with language every day."

**—Richard D. Lavoie, M.A., M.Ed.,**
former executive director of **Riverview School**, a residential school for children with learning disabilities in East Sandwich, Massachusetts. Lavoie has worked in special education since 1972 as a teacher, administrator, author, and consultant and is featured in the groundbreaking work *How Difficult Can This Be? The F.A.T. City Workshop* (PBS Video).

"This book is like reading my life's story—conflict, pain, suffering, and adaptation—and it **teaches you how to turn the agonies of a dyslexic's life into success.** It stresses the importance of the underlying need for parents to give a child love and support to build the child's self-esteem and emotional stability. As a soon-to-be grandfather with two adult dyslexic children, I believe **this book is a must read for the whole family**—because we know that 50 to 70 percent of the time learning differences run in the family."

**—Donald A. Winkler,**
former group vice president of **Ford Motor Company/chairman and CEO of Ford Motor Credit Company**, board member of the **International Dyslexic Association**, and former board member of the **National Center for Learning Disabilities**

# the secret life
## of the
# dyslexic
# child

how she thinks.

how he feels.

how they can succeed.

the
# secret life
of the
# dyslexic
# child

## robert frank, ph.d.
with kathryn e. livingston

RODALE

Produced by The Philip Lief Group, Inc.

© 2002 by The Philip Lief Group, Inc.
Cover photograph © by Yellow Dog Productions/The Image Bank/Getty Images

Printed in the United States of America
Rodale Inc. makes every effort to use acid-free ∞, recycled paper ♻.

Cover and interior design by Tara Long

**Library of Congress Cataloging-in-Publication Data**

Frank, Robert, Ph.D.
  The secret life of the dyslexic child : how she thinks, how he feels,
how they can succeed / Robert Frank with Kathryn E. Livingston.
    p.  cm.
  Includes bibliographical references and index.
  ISBN 1–57954–578–5 hardcover
  1. Dyslexic children.  I. Livingston, Kathryn E.  II. Title.
RJ496.A5 F73  2002
618.92'8553—dc21           2002006884

**Distributed to the book trade by St. Martin's Press**

2  4  6  8  10 9  7  5  3  1  hardcover

To my parents,
Jerome and Fern Frank,
my wife, Linda,
and my children, A.J. and Kevin,
and in memory of Virginia Livingston

# Contents

## Part 5: A Bright Future

# Acknowledgments

Being dyslexic, I have a lot of people to thank. I have a big support staff, who not only help me spell and write but also support me emotionally. To the Cipolla family, for coming up with the idea to write this book on New Year's Eve. To all the people at Oakton Community College who support me in one way or another, including Steven Schada, Greg Bauldauf, B. Diane Davis, Alan Rubin, the instructional support staff for their ideas and help with the book, and Nancy Stalius for reading my papers. To Elizabeth Kübler-Ross for her "Life Lessons." To Alex Posner and Andrea Voorhies for keeping me in good physical shape. To Kathy Livingston, not only for her work in writing this book with me but also for her expertise and help with the organization and ideas. To Jamie Saxon and The Philip Lief Group for working with me on the concept of this book. To Lou Cinquino at Rodale Inc. for his keen editing and insight as well as his inspiring enthusiasm throughout this project and to Rodale Inc. for publishing the book. To Sharon Silverman, who not only contributed greatly to this book, but who also helped me through graduate school. To my dad and especially my mom, whom I still call to spell for me. To my daughter, A.J., who enjoys a good "dyslexia moment" and also helps me match my clothing every morning. To my son, Kevin, for his expertise, which includes but is not limited to reading, spelling, and computing. And to my wife, Linda, who tirelessly has read my work for the last 25-some years. Love you all. And to all the dyslexic children and students I have been in contact with over the years, we can do it and this book is yours!

—R.F.


Thanks to my husband, Mitch Kriegler, and our children, Aaron, Sam, and Ben, for their support. Also thanks to Bob Frank, for his inspiration and diligence, and for once again including me on an exciting book project; to Jamie Saxon at The Philip Lief Group, for her guidance and skill; and to Lou Cinquino at Rodale for recognizing the value of this project. I'd also like to thank Sharon Silverman for her help, and my dear friend Francine Lipani for her insight.

—K.E.L.

# Introduction

As a child, I was called dumb. I was called lazy. And that was just by some of my teachers. You can imagine the names that the kids in the school yard added to that list.

As an adult, I still don't read very well. My handwriting is atrocious, and I have trouble remembering all kinds of things, from names and dates to directions and how to spell words. Yet, today, I'm a psychologist. An author. A college professor. A husband. A dad.

No, I'm not dumb or lazy. I'm dyslexic.

When I was a child, little was known about dyslexia. Remarkably, I was not even diagnosed with this learning disability until I was in graduate school. Although we have come a very long way in understanding dyslexia, I am sorry to report that some teachers and some students today still perpetuate the myths that people with dyslexia are second best or that we are unable to succeed in school and life.

Yes, a learning disability certainly introduces challenges and obstacles to success. But I assure you, with my own story as just one example, that these challenges can be met. These obstacles can be overcome.

I will show you how.

# making a difference

First and foremost, you must never lose heart. You, as parents or educators, are capable of making *the* critical difference in the life of a dyslexic child.

As I look back on my childhood, what stands out in my mind is that even though I experienced failure at school, I was treated at home by my parents as if I would find success in life. My mother worked tirelessly with me on my schoolwork, trying to understand my disability and encouraging me. As a result of her unwavering love and support, and the encouragement and confidence of my father, I began to believe that the people at school who were labeling me were wrong. I was not lazy and dumb, but rather, I was indeed a bright, creative boy who would one day achieve his dreams.

Strengthened by my inner drive—and because my parents were realistic, supportive, and dedicated—I was able to achieve my goals. With a solid education and an excellent support team, I persisted and eventually went to college, then graduate school, where I completed my dissertation. These were achievements that my elementary and high school teachers, for the most part, would never have believed possible. In fact, my high school guidance counselor suggested I pursue a job as a gas station attendant after high school and forget about college. My parents, however, refused to lower their expectations for me. They believed I could achieve, and so, together, we never gave up on my dreams.

The foundation for success in life is laid down in childhood. Whether you realize it or not, *your reaction and response to your child's dyslexia* can make the difference between whether your child will

confidently down the road toward success or be sidetracked
on the back road of failure in his life. Make no mistake, having
dyslexia involves struggle either way, but with your love, consistent
support, and involvement, the outcome can and will be positive for
your child. The way you teach, the way you support, and the manner
in which you react to and help manage this disability will dramatically impact your child's success in life.

## understanding your child

So, how can you make the difference? While it requires love, it takes
much more than that alone. It takes more than tutors or manuals. It
takes more than phonics courses and books on tape. What it takes
most of all is understanding.

In working with dyslexic children in my private practice—and in
king back on how my parents helped me manage my dyslexia—I
come to realize that understanding is the all-important first step
her experts and specialists overlook. In order to establish a pos-
oductive relationship with your dyslexic child, you must first
nd his secret life. Until a parent gains this crucial under-
ll the strategies in the world will be of little consequence.
anding your child unlocks the door to helping your child.
e for her each day? What is it like to see the world
es? To think how she thinks? To feel what he's feeling?
erstand this secret life, you can better partner with your
l him to success.

## the veil of secrecy

nside this secret world? How can you as a parent see the
ur child does in order to better understand her fears and
s and needs?

It may be difficult for you to even begin to imagine what your dyslexic child might be going through each day. But this secret world will come to life vividly in the pages of this book. You will begin to see and feel how the dyslexic child experiences the world quite differently than other kids. Dyslexia is not just about mixing up letters or reading slowly. I will present many scenarios that describe a dyslexic child's life; in some you will see your child, and in others you won't. But as we move through each chapter, you will gain an increasing understanding of what it is like to live with this disability every day and to encounter its effects in so many areas—from learning a locker combination to reading aloud in class to riding a bike to the park on your own.

In order to help your child, it is so important to thoroughly immerse yourself in what life is like for him. Throughout the book, I've included dozens of everyday scenarios that illustrate the myriad ways dyslexia comes into play in your child's world. These scenarios are presented in the context of practical strategies you can use to set goals and to deal with the challenges the dyslexic child encounters each and every day. Understand that dyslexia affects your child's life from the moment he gets up until the moment he goes to bed at nigh. The approaches and practical tips in the coming chapters will hel you and your child identify and use the tools that make living wi dyslexia more manageable and less frustrating for both of you.

As I look at the dyslexic child's life at home, at school, and in outside world, I also describe strategies you as a parent (or educa can use to help your child (or student) cope with and manage his ability. Although these strategies will help your child, it's essenti understand that there is no cure for dyslexia. As I discuss in ch. 1, dyslexia is a neurologically based disability. As science make: inroads, no doubt we will learn more and more about dysl causes, but it's necessary to accept that dyslexia is a lifelong tion that is most effectively addressed through realistic goals and smart, proven strategies. There is no magic pill your child can take to make it go away.

# living the secret life

People often ask me why other experts and specialists have not discovered this secret life. I believe it is because they themselves are not dyslexic. They are practitioners trained to come up with solutions. Most are trained in school only to give strategies, to "fix" the dyslexic child. Through no fault of their own, they don't comprehend the kind of reality the dyslexic child lives in because they are not dyslexic.

Because of my dyslexia, this book is not like other books you may read on the subject. The truth of the matter is that not many people with dyslexia write books—it's just not something most of us endeavor to do. With the help of a writer and an editor, however, I have been able to organize and express my ideas for publication. And because of my dyslexia, I can help you understand your child's world in a way that few other experts can.

I see the world as a dyslexic adult, and I have known the world the way dyslexic children do. And you can, too. It takes only an open mind and an open heart. Let's begin now to deeply understand what dyslexia really means to your child as we look into this secret life and open the door to a brighter future for your family.

the secret life

# part 1

# 1. What Is Going On inside My Child's Mind?

**Not long ago,** I attended a seminar for professionals in the area of educational psychology, which is my specialty. As we entered the classroom, the seminar leaders handed each participant a pamphlet and informed us that we'd each be asked to read a segment aloud as part of the day's discussion.

I was amazed on that day to find the same sense of fear pulsing through my body that I had felt as an 8-year-old child being asked to read aloud in class. Even as an adult with a Ph.D., I take my learning disability everywhere, every day of my life. Each day, I must learn to deal with it again; dyslexia is a secret I carry with me wherever I go.

As I awaited my short presentation, I recalled the terror I felt as a child when my turn to read approached and the embarrassment I inevitably felt as I stumbled slowly over the words, often missing the main point of what I had read. All these years later, my focus once again was on my own struggle with reading rather than listening to the content of the readers who came before me. Once again, because of my dyslexia, I ran the risk of totally missing the point of what we were doing at that time in the seminar due to my fear and doubt about my own ability to perform a simple task. But the challenges of dyslexia go far beyond reading.

## much more than a reading problem

There are many subcategories that fall under the learning disabilities umbrella; dyslexia is one of them and there are many others. If your child is diagnosed with a learning disability, it does not necessarily mean that he is dyslexic. Too many people mistakenly believe that dyslexia is simply a matter of reversing numbers or having difficulty reading; it is much more complex and far-reaching than that. Dyslexia is also difficulty with writing, spatial relations, directions, time management, word recall, and memory. It is the inability to recall for a moment your best friend's last name; it is the panic of knowing that at any moment in any day, mind blurriness could kick in. The emotional toll that stems from loss of memory, especially, can be great. Your child may be too young to articulate this sense of dread, but as he grows older, he will become increasingly aware of dyslexia's many manifestations.

Although dyslexia is a word that sounds familiar to many, there is quite a bit of confusion about what it really means. At its most basic level, the word dyslexia comes from the Greek *dys* meaning poor and *lexia* meaning language. Taking it a step further, dyslexia is a neurological problem that relates to language and reading skills; spelling, writing, listening, speaking, and memory skills may also be impacted.

It's important to note that while we can pull a convenient definition from a book, as a parent you must approach the meaning of dyslexia from the perspective of your own child's experiences—and this, in part, is why it is so essential that you understand how dyslexia affects your child as an individual.

Yes, all dyslexics exhibit some difficulty with language skills, but what that means from child to child may vary greatly. Your child may have a great deal of difficulty with reading, yet he might not reverse numbers or have memory problems. Or perhaps he reads adequately enough but spells or writes with an inordinate amount of struggle. I find that most books present dyslexia in black-and-white terms; as a result, many parents may chalk it up to a definition as simple as "somebody who reverses letters or has trouble reading." Since this disability is much more complex, I doubt very much that there will ever be a remedy that will work the same way for every child.

## how to know if your child has dyslexia

Most often, the clues don't crystallize until your child begins to read. Even then, it may take some time before dyslexia can be clearly diagnosed. (In some severe cases, there are signs that appear even before reading begins, such as delayed speech.) Up until age 6 or 7, it's not unusual for kids to reverse letters and words when they read or write, but by the time your child is 8, these signs may signal a deeper problem. By the third grade, diagnostic tests can reveal whether your child is dyslexic. These tests (which we'll discuss in more depth in chapter 8) are usually administered after a child has exhibited a persistent problem with reading. A school or private testing facility can determine if your child is dyslexic through a test of reading ability (speed, decoding, memory, and comprehension) and a test of overall intellectual ability (IQ). Experts will also recommend that your child be examined to rule out any medical, visual, or auditory problems.

As a parent, you may sense your child is not "keeping up" long before anyone else. You may notice one or more of the following clues.

- Low self-esteem
- Spelling difficulties
- Difficulty reading aloud
- Mixing up of left and right
- Problems following directions
- Slow completion of written assignments
- Difficulty with math
- Reluctance to go to school

Keep in mind that dyslexia is an "invisible" disability, but that doesn't mean your child won't feel as if his dyslexia is obvious to anyone who glances his way. In truth, no one can point to dyslexia the way you can to a broken leg; there are no overt signs that will differentiate your child from any other. Because of this, I believe, the dyslexic child experiences his "secret life" in a unique way. He is well aware that he is not like other kids but may be quite committed to keeping a veil of secrecy over his disability.

# what dyslexia isn't

Even though dyslexia affects your child's ability to read, spell, understand language, or express herself clearly while writing or speaking, it's not due to lack of intelligence. Most dyslexic individuals are of average or above average intelligence. Unfortunately, a child's problems with the ability to learn and to process, retain, retrieve, and express information can result in the mistaken impression that the child isn't "smart." In the past, dyslexic kids, including me, were often labeled dumb or lazy.

Today, we know that this is far from true; in fact, a study conducted at the University of Washington revealed that dyslexic kids use nearly five times more brain area than normal children while performing a simple language task. Far from "lazy," the brains of dyslexic kids actually work on overdrive. It is very important that parents, educators, and health professionals get the message that dyslexic children expend a great deal of energy just to get through the day; laziness or lack of intelligence has nothing to do with the problem.

# who gets dyslexia

Here is another topic that may lend itself to misinterpretation. While experts claim that dyslexia affects about 15 percent of the United States population, I suspect that the numbers are slightly higher because some kids remain undiagnosed during their childhood and well into adulthood—and some are never correctly diagnosed. Although there is much less "slipping through the cracks" in schools now than even 10 years ago, I'm sure that there are still some school districts that lag in making proper diagnostic efforts.

For adults who pursue careers that don't involve much reading or writing, it's quite possible they've been able to keep their dyslexia under wraps for years. Old Aunt Betty, who can't spell worth a dime, and your college buddy Charlie, who runs a shoe factory and employs several assistants to do his paperwork, may very well be dyslexics that no one has formally identified. One man I know runs a lucrative business and sits on his town planning board. He habitually spells words wrong, reverses or omits letters, and seems to exhibit many of the signs of dyslexia. He has never been diagnosed and, with a shrug, chalks his deficits up to "a poor school system." He simply avoids reading and writing as much as he can.

So, who gets dyslexia? Anyone, from any ethnic background or socioeconomic status and of either gender. There is no means to predict if a certain child will have dyslexia. However, if someone in your family has dyslexia, your child has a higher chance of getting it than if the condition doesn't appear anywhere in your family. A genetic link may exist within a family, but a dyslexic parent won't necessarily have a dyslexic child (neither of my children is dyslexic, for example). However, my uncle has the disability, and it is possible that one of my kids could have a child with dyslexia. Dyslexia is neurologically based and often familial; individuals may inherit the genetic link from an immediate family member—if your parent, spouse, aunt, uncle, brother, or sister is dyslexic, you *might* have a dyslexic child.

# what is different about the dyslexic brain

Although various theories regarding the origin of dyslexia have been presented over the years, recent use of magnetic resonance imaging (MRI) has allowed researchers to delve more deeply into the causes. Sally E. Shaywitz, M.D., of the Yale University School of Medicine, has used MRI technology to examine computer-generated images of the brain while it is performing intellectual tasks. She found that dyslexic readers showed reduced activity in the angular gyrus—the area of the brain that links the visual cortex and visual association area to the language areas.

In addition, Dr. Shaywitz found that when reading, dyslexics exhibit greater activity in a part of the brain called Broca's area than non-dyslexics. This suggests that dyslexics may employ this brain region to compensate for deficits in the brain regions normally employed for phonological skills (the ability to identify and manipulate individual language sounds). According to Dr. Shaywitz, dyslexic readers have difficulty with breaking spoken words into their component sounds and the ability to match these letter sounds to the letters that represent them.

What does all this mean to your child? In a nutshell, brain

imaging technology allows researchers to examine the area of the brain that is affected by dyslexia—and perhaps, to finally put to rest some myths regarding the source of the problem. With this new knowledge in hand, researchers can continue to explore the roots of dyslexia and possibly offer methods to help kids learn more effectively. The underlying fact that dyslexia is a neurological problem, however, cannot be ignored. Your child will not "grow out" of dyslexia, but with your consistent, involved support and encouragement, she can learn to live with her disability and succeed as I have.

# dyslexia in daily life

What impact will dyslexia have on your child? That depends on the severity of his dyslexia as well as upon how effective and supportive you are in helping him confront the problem.

Here are several ways dyslexia may manifest itself in your child's daily life.

## Word Recall

My children often joke with me when I can't recall a word, and as an adult, I can usually see the humor in my situation. I'm apt to say, "Kevin, get the watchamacallit and put it in the thingamajig" because I just can't come up with simple words such as "laundry" and "hamper." The wiring of the dyslexic brain can lend itself to this sort of problem. Everyone experiences these lapses now and then (non-dyslexic adults sometimes wryly call this word mix-up "having a senior moment"), but for the dyslexic, these lapses may be much more frequent and more troublesome.

When a dyslexic child is asked to write a story or letter, oftentimes she can't think of the word she wants to use or can't figure out how to spell it. A simple word like "only" or "their" may present a problem. When I'm writing and can't think of a word, I often try to replace it with a word I can spell or that will substitute. This not only slows me down but risks the choice of a word that isn't as effective. Imagine your child's frustration when she has to stop repeatedly because of problems with word recall.

## The Time Factor

As a college professor, I'm often asked to contact people or send information here or there. Simple tasks such as addressing a letter can eat up my morning, because I may not know how to spell a simple name like Marsha or I may be baffled by the spelling of a street name. I'm likely to pull out all my directories and telephone books searching for words that most people can grasp within seconds. Imagine the time this takes.

When I was in graduate school, I was in a study group that met two or three times a week. Whenever we'd get together, my classmates would all be impressed at how well I seemed to know the material. I studied very hard—many more hours than any of the other students—and when we'd discuss our assignments, I would invariably be the most knowledgeable student in the group.

Naturally, the other students were all mystified when they would get A's and I would only get B's on the exams. "How in the world did you get only a B?" they'd ask incredulously. I'd throw up my hands. Sometimes, the material I thought I knew so well would evade me when I sat down to write about it on an exam; other times, I'd miss the thrust of the essay question and lose a lot of points there. Sometimes, I suspected, my professors were simply turned off by my handwriting itself, which appears childlike since I don't print neatly and never write in cursive, and would mark me down for that. In any case, the other students would always do better than I did, even though I seemed to know the material inside out the night before the exam and even though I had studied much longer and more diligently than my friends.

At times, I wondered if my high-school guidance counselor had been right when he had suggested that I pursue a job as a gas station attendant and forget about college. But I had other aspirations—and luckily, a supportive family—and was determined to succeed in spite of my dyslexia. Today, I know dozens of successful professionals, many with master's and doctoral degrees, who have managed their dyslexia in successful ways so that their academic and professional goals were not thwarted. Some of these people are therapists like me; one's a clinical psychologist. I know physicians and even a librarian who are dyslexic. The achievements of all these professionals would certainly have surprised my guidance counselor.

It's important to understand that everything takes longer for the dyslexic child: writing, spelling, reading, following directions, studying. She has to work harder than her classmates. Even if she uses all the coping strategies available, it will still take her longer than most other people to complete her work. A simple task like looking up a number in the phone book can become an aggravating chore for the dyslexic child or adult. To the child, the task can seem insurmountably frustrating. And to you, the length of time that it takes your child to complete the task can be remarkably frustrating as well. But remember: Your child is not lazy. She is not unintelligent. Her brain is working even harder than yours—it's just taking her longer to get the answers. With your confidence and support, however, she will find them.

## A Sense of Disorganization

It can be frightening for a child to be constantly unsure if what he has heard is correct or if what he has read is what the words really say.

Aaron, a boy I know, told me he was in downtown Chicago one day with his mom. They were going to a favorite restaurant—one they frequented often—and he was leading the way. Suddenly, his mother stopped dead in her tracks and asked what in the world he was doing. Apparently, Aaron had taken a wrong turn, even though he had walked that route with his mom more than a hundred times.

Even simple concepts like *later, before, previously,* or *left* and *right* can be baffling to a dyslexic child when he first hears them. He needs time to process these ideas. Imagine if you went down the street to mail a letter in a post box you had used for 20 years, and suddenly you weren't sure whether it was on the left or right corner of the street. Or you were certain it was on the right, but it was actually on the left. The phrases, words, and directions that we use to organize our world can be confusing to a dyslexic child; he must work harder to sort them out and make sense of his surroundings.

As an adult, I can laugh at my errors and work them out (in fact, for the older dyslexic child and adult, a sense of humor in itself is vitally important). Once, I was looking for an address that would have put me in the middle of a lake if it had even existed at all. I had simply reversed some numbers. But think what this is like for a child. The constant uncertainty about directions and numbers can be very disorienting. "Why can't I do it?" the child wonders. "Why can't I get to the right place at the right time?" One boy told me, "Dyslexia just makes me want to hit my head!"

## Mind Blurriness

Many dyslexics live in a world that can best be described as mentally blurry. To help parents of children in my practice understand what this is like, I ask them to think about a time when they were just so tired they couldn't think straight, when it was hopeless to even concentrate on one task because it just blurred into all the things that were crowding their mind. This is mind blurriness. You may have it once in a while, when you've been working too long at something or when you get a couple nights of poor sleep. For the dyslexic child, even the well-rested one, his secret life is like this much of the time.

## The Memory Stumbling Block

I have found that difficulty with memory—both short-term and long-term—is one of the most emotionally painful aspects of dyslexia. It's impossible for me to remember certain experiences from my past—there are many precious days I spent raising my two children as a stay-at-home dad, for instance, that I just can't recall. When a non-dyslexic person stores something in his brain, it's filed away fairly neatly, as if it's been slipped into a file in his computer. When I store information, however, I may put it in one file in my brain, only to find that it's mysteriously gone when I try to retrieve it. My file is one big one without categories or subheadings; a non-dyslexic's filing system is more elaborate and detailed, making retrieval easier. Tracking information down can take me a very long time. It's in there all right but not where I thought I put it!

As a college professor, I've taught Psychology 101 countless times, yet every time I teach the course, I must reactivate my brain in order to locate and reorganize the material. In a way, this is good, because the information always seems exciting and fresh to me (and hopefully to my students as well). Still, I must spend an extraordinary amount of time remastering and reorganizing material I should know by heart.

Remembering names, reciting the presidents in order, or even locating a drinking fountain in a hallway he's been down 50 times can pose a real problem for the dyslexic child. Imagine how a 10-year-old boy feels when he can't tell a new friend he's met at soccer camp what his phone number is or how frustrated a 13-year-old girl feels when she jumbles up an e-mail address while trying to contact her friend about plans for the weekend.

## Good Morning, Bad Afternoon

As you become more attuned to understanding the secret life of your dyslexic child, you will be able to help him identify the parts of the day when his brain works best, as well as the periods when nothing he does seems to work very well. I know I work most efficiently in the morning. As the day wears on, my spelling deteriorates, and my mind blurriness takes over. You may find your child works best later in the day. To be most helpful to your child, you need to help him find when he works best, a process I'll discuss in more detail in later chapters.

It's important to remember that, as with most kids, children with dyslexia function best with a good night's sleep. Feelings of disorganization are intensified when a child with dyslexia stays up too late and doesn't follow a healthy bedtime routine. I'm in bed by 10:00 at the latest each night and rise at 5:00 A.M. Through many years of living with dyslexia, I've discovered that my days go better when I fully utilize the morning hours. On the occasions when I must stay up later (for instance, I serve on our local school board and am often required to attend meetings that can last very late into the night), my productivity on the following day suffers.

# dysfunction that does not go away

The other day, a dear friend called to see if my wife, Linda, and I were planning to attend a party arranged by some of our former college classmates. I suggested to my friend, Mary, that she drive down from Peoria, spend the night at our home, and go with us to Mary's for the party. Mary, who has known me for 20-some years, calmly responded, "No, Bob. I'll be driving *up* from Peoria, and then we'll be driving to *Jeanne's* together. I'm Mary."

I laughed at my mistake; of course I knew I was talking to Mary, but I still can't tell you whether Peoria is north or south of Glenview, where I live, because that's the kind of information that just gets mixed and muddled as it travels through my brain. I bring up this little anecdote not to bore you with my social calendar but to point out that the brain of a dyslexic individual is very quirky. I don't believe that there will ever be a pill or a magic potion that will "cure" these unpredictable mix-ups for me.

As we discover more about dyslexia, our methods of learning to manage it will continue to improve. However, dyslexia is a condition that your child will always live with. While there's really no altering the "hardwiring" of the brain, once you understand how dyslexia affects your child, you will be able to help her develop ways to cope with it. The key is understanding how dyslexia affects your own child; then you can begin to develop the support systems and strategies she will be able to use for life. The good thing about this is, once you've identified and refined the problems that dyslexia causes for your child, you'll know what you're dealing with, and you will be able to work with your child to find creative, workable solutions that will meet her needs—in childhood, during the teen years, and as an adult.

I live a great life. I have wonderful experiences, friends, family, and associates, but I do have to deal with my dyslexia on a daily basis. At times, I feel discouraged that I must live with dyslexia, but for the most part, I've found ways to manage my disability and enjoy life immensely. In the following chapters, I hope to share these methods and strategies with you so that you can help your child reach her full potential, too.

# 2. What Is Going On inside My Child's Heart?

**A few years back,** one of my prize students, a young man who was majoring in psychology, confessed to me that he was unsure if he should continue his college studies because he was afraid he might be "found out." Mike was an A student who did excellent work in all of his classes, but because he was dyslexic, he had to work very hard indeed to achieve his high grades. He revealed to me that he couldn't remember much of the foundational knowledge he was supposed to know as a psych major. His greatest fear, he said, was that one day someone would knock on his door and announce he'd been discovered to be dyslexic and that he was to leave the college. Each day, he faced the fear that the discovery of his learning disability would destroy his hopes and aspirations.

Mike was a smart kid, and I knew he was going to be okay, but I saw a great deal of sadness in his face when he talked about his dyslexia. I could tell that he was thinking, "Why me? Is this ever going to get any better?" The reality is he's not going to get "better," in the sense that one gets better from the flu, but I knew he would find ways to succeed. In fact, he had already, by finding someone like me to include in his support system and with whom he could be comfortable enough to be open and honest about his dyslexia.

The fear of discovery is perhaps the most significant element of the dyslexic child's secret life and the emotion that needs the deepest understanding by parents. Dyslexia can't be seen. It's not like a broken leg that requires a cast, and often a child will try to keep his disability a secret. I know dyslexic adults who actually try to avoid all public situations that involve reading, writing, spelling, speaking aloud, or remembering, which is nearly impossible to do in our society. Yet many dyslexics can be quite creative about ways to circumvent these tasks.

# feelings of fear

You may not even realize this, but there's a good chance that your dyslexic child lives in fear. It's a fear that afflicts all children at one time or another—the fear of not fitting in.

For children with learning disabilities, it's a fear that doesn't just go away without some attention. Here's how you can help.

### "I'm Afraid They'll Make Fun of Me"

*Daniel, a seventh grader, knows that the class will be asked to read aloud from the play* The Miracle Worker *at 10 o'clock in the morning. At quarter of 10, he suddenly begins throwing spitballs across the room at a classmate. It's just a matter of time before the teacher, Mrs. Stein, notices his behavior and sends him into the hall to sit on the bench. For now, Daniel has won. He's spared the experience of reading aloud in front of his classmates. Even though Daniel's classmates know he has a learning disability, they aren't quite sophisticated enough to connect his acting out to the day's reading schedule or mature enough not to make fun of him.*

Often, the child with dyslexia finds himself in situations in which those around him are unaware of his disability, so he may decide to keep his problem under wraps because he feels ashamed, embarrassed, or "not normal." This places a tremendous amount of pressure on the child, who is perpetually wondering, "When will I be found out?" The only solution, he may feel, is to avoid situations in which he may be "discovered." Shying away from the drama club, skipping a day of school or feigning illness when there's a spelling test, and walking off the playground when the kids who are jumping rope start reciting rhymes are just a few of the ways that a dyslexic child—just like a dyslexic adult—attempts to avoid uncomfortable situations in which his "secret" may be divulged.

Sometimes, parents don't acknowledge these fears as real. But the fear of discovery is a complex web you must navigate with your child. If you are to help, you must gain an understanding of your child's sensitivity to the issue of discovery.

In order to help parents understand this issue, I sometimes present a battery of questions. I ask the parent: Would you be afraid to go to the grocery store and write out a check to pay? Would you be afraid to drive to a new town and find an address? Would you be afraid to fill out a medical form at a doctor's office? Would you be afraid to follow directions to get to a store in town?

Usually, the parent answers "No" or "Of course not!" to these questions. When I explain that even as a dyslexic adult with a Ph.D., I can find many of these situations frightening, they begin to raise their eyebrows. For instance, I tell them, there is one neighborhood not far from my house where I simply cannot drive. The streets are so confusing that I'm bound to get lost there and never find my way home. Recently, while I was in-line skating with Alex, a friend of mine, he joked that I'd surely be lost if he sped out ahead. I agreed but added, "You can leave me here, but I'll just make a new friend." As an adult, I'd be quick to seek help when I was lost; a child might not be so willing or so capable of finding help and asking for directions.

I then take it a step further and ask the parents if they think their child might be afraid to read aloud in class, to ride his bike to the park, to play a complicated board game with friends, and so forth. Usually, the parents will answer yes to many of these questions. As we delve more deeply into the fear that their child may be feeling, the parents begin to realize that the child is afraid to read aloud not only because he will sound "stupid" but also because he will be "discovered." The underlying fear in all of these situations is that someone will find out you are dyslexic, and your disability will be exposed. No one wants others to know "bad" things about him.

Many children, even many adults, fear that once their disability is out in the open, they will not be able to do what they hoped and believed they could do. This couldn't be further from the truth. But just like my student Mike, who got A's in college, many dyslexics believe that when others discover the nature of their disability, they will no longer be allowed to continue to go to college, work at a prestigious job, be accepted by peers, and so on.

The emotional toll that this fear takes can be overwhelming, and that is why it is so important to confront this fear with your child and to help him find ways to cope with his disability. I could easily sit in my house all day and worry about whether I will get lost as I drive in my car, whether I'll get in an accident and have to fill out a report, whether I'll spend hours wandering the grocery store because I can't remember the name of a product, and whether all these things will cause me to lose everything I've worked so hard for if anyone finds out. I know this fear of discovery is unrealistic, and I'm not likely to lose anything at all if my dyslexia is revealed. Nevertheless, this is a very real fear that is deeply embedded in a dyslexic individual's secret life and casts a dark shadow over every day.

The other choice I can make—and the one I do make every day—is to get up in the morning, use my compensating strategies to get through the day, get the things done I need to get done, and maintain a positive attitude. The most important point for parents to understand is that the fear can be crippling, more crippling than the disability itself.

Encourage your child to talk about his fears. He needs to know that you won't laugh at him or downplay his worries. Even if his fears or concerns seem inflated to you, they are very real to him. Shrugging them off or saying, "Oh, don't worry about that so much—you'll do fine," is a big mistake. Instead, listen to your child, hear him out fully, and then talk about strategies and ways of handling new situations. Let your child know that he can come to you at any time to talk about what's troubling him. As a dyslexic adult, I can assure you that your child's fears are very real. With your support and encouragement, however, they can be managed.

# feelings of frustration

The feelings of frustration your child experiences as he negotiates his life with dyslexia can take many forms—common feelings that will resurface time and time again as he approaches his schoolwork and interacts with peers and family. Helping your child cope with and manage feelings of frustration is one of the most important arenas where parents can make a difference. Here are some areas that may present your child with a sense of frustration as he attempts to face daily challenges, both socially and academically.

### "I Can't Remember Words"

*Six-year-old Billy is bright and energetic, but sometimes his mom, Sue, wonders what in the world he's talking about. He loves to ride his bike up and down the driveway in front of the house, but today, he tells his mom,*

*"Can you get me the, you know, the thing you keep in the place back there?" Sue is at a loss. Why can't Billy remember a word as simple as "bike"? She's determined not to open the garage until he says what he means. But Billy is stumbling and searching for words so frantically that Sue finally gives in and gets his bike out. She can't bear to watch her child struggle so fiercely.*

Many dyslexic children and adults have problems with word recall. As I explained earlier, the information is stored in the brain, but retrieval presents a problem. For the dyslexic child, the time it takes to recall a simple word can be extremely frustrating. As kids grow older, this inability to call up words (referred to as dysnomia) can cause embarrassment or feelings of inadequacy. In addition, others may become angry or embarrassed at the dyslexic's inability; my kids sometimes lose patience with me when I can't remember simple terms. Parents may lose patience with their dyslexic child when simple words just won't come. This just compounds the child's feelings of frustration and inferiority.

## "Everything Takes Me Longer"

*Tina's mom has reminded her to write her grandmother a thank-you note for the surprise birthday party she gave Tina at her house in the country. She had invited six 10-year-old girls for a sleepover in her beautiful Victorian house. But when Tina sits down to write the letter, the words just won't come to her, and she knows her mother is getting annoyed. Tina can't even spell the word "surprised," so she has substituted the word "shocked," but that doesn't really sound right. She's been sitting at the desk for nearly an hour and has written only one sentence. Tina really wants to write her grandmother a nice note, but it takes so long! While she sits trying, she is missing an important scout meeting, but her mom won't let her go until she is finished writing.*

Writing a thank-you note can be a difficult chore for the dyslexic child or adult. It's nice to write a thank-you note in longhand; certainly, it's more personal than a typed note. But the dyslexic may find herself scratching out words, erasing, substituting, and generally making a mess of things. As the clock ticks away and the dyslexic struggles with this seemingly simple task, she may begin to question her abilities and intelligence, wondering, "Why does it take me so much longer than everyone else to do the simplest thing?" Again, frustration and tension mount as the dyslexic child realizes she is missing out on other activities because an ordinary chore takes so much time.

## "I'm So Disorganized"

*Vincent is up in his room working on a homework assignment. He has to write a paragraph in response to a news story about the possible discovery of water on Mars and what it might mean if there were life on another planet. He scribbles out a few sentences, reads them, and crumples up the paper. He repeats the same thing two more times. Then he pulls out his math notebook and works on a few problems, but he's forgotten his calculator at school and can't seem to get the right answers. Then, feeling totally frustrated, he kicks his wastebasket, stomps out of his room, and goes downstairs to turn on the TV.*

The disorganization some dyslexics experience can lead to feelings of confusion and despair. When the dyslexic child can't find his focus or when his mind wanders, it's difficult to complete a simple task before moving on to the next. Sometimes, the child may not even realize he's jumped from task to task until much later. It can be alarming to suddenly realize that you've left a task without even knowing it. I was shocked and frightened to find one day that I'd left a burner lit on the stove and hadn't even realized it. This could happen to anyone, of course, but when I make such a mistake, I begin to worry that my dyslexia could cause me to make a serious or dangerous error. When a child experiences this sense of fear and self-doubt, it can be almost paralyzing.

## "My Mind Is Blurry"

*Ethan, a 12-year-old, often sits down to do his homework, gets up to go on-line, and then runs outside to play basketball. When his mom comes home from work and finds him in the driveway shooting hoops, she asks if he's finished his homework, and he has to admit, "I forgot." For some reason, Ethan just can't stay focused long enough to finish a task. It takes so much concentration and effort to finish a single worksheet that he often loses in-terest and patience, jumps up to do something else, and then forgets what he was doing in the first place.*

Like disorganization, the "mind blurriness" that sets in can cause a child to feel confused and unfocused. The blurriness can feel worse at certain times of the day. After school, some kids may need time to blow off some steam before they sit down to do their homework. In Ethan's case, it might have been better if he'd gone outside to play, had dinner, and then sat down to tackle his homework with a fresh outlook.

## "I Forget"

*Eleven-year-old Derrick is totally stuck. His camp counselor has told him to take 15 minutes to clean up his bunk, stop by the swimming hole and pick up some life preservers for the canoe from one of the other counselors, and then report back to the mess hall and help set up for breakfast. Der-rick is stymied. He just can't remember what he's supposed to do. He's standing outside the lean-to when his counselor spots him. "What the heck are you waiting for?" he calls out.*

Sometimes, it seems as if the dyslexic child is extraordinarily forgetful. It's not that Derrick has forgotten what his camp counselor said, however, but that he hasn't had the time to process the information. While he is absorbing the first part of the direction to clean up his bunk, he has not been able to process the second and third directions to get some life preservers and then help set up for breakfast. Derrick is left with a frustrating sense that he has forgotten something, when in fact he has simply not yet had a chance to process the words.

Often, when a teacher gives directions, a child will ask to have them repeated. The teacher may respond, "But I already told them to you." Instead of asking to have the teacher repeat the directions, what the child really means is, "You said it in a way I didn't understand." Feelings of frustration and inadequacy again surface, along with the frightening sense of "forgetfulness" that is really a manifestation of the brain's inability to process information quickly.

## "I'm Having a Bad Day"

*Jenna, a ninth grader, is standing at the bus stop waiting for her friends. She's beginning to think she's made a mistake, since the only other person at the stop is an old lady in a pink raincoat. She could have sworn Amanda said to meet at the stop bus number 167 comes to, but maybe Amanda said the 176 stop, which is two blocks in the other direction. It's all so confusing. Jenna sighs. She's irritated with Amanda for giving her the wrong information. Now she'll miss her day out with her friends. She's certainly having a bad day.*

Jenna isn't sure if she's made a mistake or if Amanda has steered her wrong. Often, the dyslexic individual blames others, believing that her own confusion is the result of others' errors. When she gets home and reconnects with Amanda, she'll learn that she'd been given the right information but had mixed it up. Realizing this, Jenna will then feel angry at herself and saddened that her disability has caused her to miss out on a day of fun with her peers.

It may take many years before the dyslexic child begins to realize that things that happen on a "bad day" are sometimes the result of her disability. Instead, she may be utterly convinced that she is at the right bus stop, that she should have turned left instead of right, or that she has a correct address when she's actually confused the numbers. The realization that the mistake is hers can lead to feelings of inferiority and loss: Why can't I get it right? Why can't I be in the right place at the right time? Why does this have to happen to me?

# isolation

As kids get older and more self-sufficient, it's natural for parents to give them more autonomy to let them pursue their own interests. But parents of children with learning disabilities must pay close attention as this begins to happen. Is your child really just removing himself from situations because of embarrassment or fear? He may stand to gain from associating with other children who share his interests and challenges.

## "Just Leave Me Alone"

*Nine-year-old Frankie stops into the library to drop off a book for his mom while she idles her car outside the entry. As he approaches the counter, he notices a group of his friends from school gathered around a table near the computers. They all have books on the table and are drawing pictures. When the librarian looks up and notices Frankie standing hesitantly by the counter, she calls out, "Hi there! Would you like to join our summer reading group?" Frankie shakes his head and races back out the door.*

A hollow sense of isolation and loneliness is common among children with dyslexia. There are so many activities other kids enjoy freely that they would have difficulty mastering that it's often easier simply to back away. When I was a child, my mother signed me up for a Junior Great Books club. Several of my friends had joined, and for them, the reading of the classics was a pleasure. Needless to say, Junior Great Books was an unmitigated disaster for me. It made me realize that I would never be like other kids when it came to reading.

It may help to join a support group with other dyslexic kids and their parents. Even though your child needs to learn how to operate and excel in the world of non-dyslexics, it will also be comforting for him, at times, to be with other children who share similar worries, challenges, and experiences.

# two paths ahead

With the diagnosis of dyslexia, you and your child face a fork in the road. If you take the path of offering consistent support, taking the responsibility to learn as much as you can about dyslexia, and identifying and practicing creative solutions and strategies, you will be able to help your child manage his dyslexia, achieve success, and pursue his dreams.

If you take the opposite path, however—the path of indifference, shame, or denial—you leave your child lost in this world without the powerful emotional and practical support parents can give that can make a crucial difference in the outcome of a child's life. Here's a look at the direction each path can take. Each anecdote paints a vastly different picture of a dyslexic child's potential and achievement.

## The Powerful Path of Emotional Support

*Ella, a 10-year-old, is practicing riding her bike to the park around the corner. Her parents, Steve and Madelaine, are very supportive and have* coached Ella carefully. They want to help her gain her independence, yet they are aware that Ella has many fears. In particular, Ella has a great deal of difficulty in distinguishing between her right and her left. Madelaine has bought Ella a bright new watch to wear on her left wrist. She has explained to Ella repeatedly that the watch is worn on the left and that she can use it as a clue when a teacher says "turn left at the drinking fountain" or when a game requires you to put your right foot into the circle first.

As Ella readies for her bike ride, her father patiently reminds her to use her clue when she gets to the corner. He will walk behind, at a distance, he tells his daughter, so she needn't be afraid if she makes a mistake. He watches as Ella stops at the corner and checks her wrists. She turns left and continues to the park. When Steve arrives, he waves at Ella and tells her she did a great job. He'll be back in 10 minutes, he says, to help her prepare for the bike ride home.

When he arrives back at the park, Steve will patiently explain to Ella that she now needs to reverse the direction and check her right wrist to remember to turn right on the way home. Over time, Ella will develop this and other clues to help her with her sense of direction. Throughout, her parents will be patient guides and teachers. They realize that in order for Ella to develop a sense of confidence and overcome her fears, they must give her a supportive base. Because they understand that Ella's disability causes confusion about directions, they never blame their daughter or make her feel ashamed. Instead, they schedule extra time to prepare Ella for new situations and work together to find creative solutions that will help her.

## The Painful Path of Emotional Distance

Matty, an 11-year-old boy, has been asked to mail a letter and then pick up a box of macaroni and cheese at the corner grocery store. His parents, Glenda and Jack, are busy real estate agents, and neither has the patience *or time to work with Matty on his learning disability; they are leaving it up to the school. When Matty arrives at the store, he stands in front of the pasta aisle for a good 15 minutes. There are at least four different brands of packaged macaroni and cheese, and he can't remember which is the right one. Finally, he grabs any box and heads for the checkout. He's sure that his parents will be mad that he's taken so long.*

*When Matty comes home with the wrong box of macaroni and cheese, his mother is annoyed. "Why don't you ever listen?" she snaps. When she notices the letter in his hand, she really loses her temper. "Matty, I told you to mail that letter first! Why don't you pay attention? Didn't you hear a word I said?"*

Unfortunately for Matty, his parents are not making the necessary effort to understand what dyslexia means for their child. If they had, they might have shown Matty a picture of the box they wanted. A coupon or ad cut from a magazine would have helped Matty identify the proper box of macaroni and cheese, or an empty box could have been retrieved from recycling to serve as a reminder before he set out. Since his mom wanted him to complete two tasks, she could have repeated the directions several times and then asked Matty to repeat back to her what she wanted before he started off. That way, he might have been more likely to have remembered that the letter also needed to be mailed.

Over time, Matty will have a much more difficult time dealing with his dyslexia than will Ella, simply because Ella has the backup and support of her parents, on both a practical and an emotional level. While Ella is offered the time, patience, and strategies necessary to succeed at everyday tasks, Matty is almost guaranteed to fail. The pressure and shame that his parents place upon him will only lead to more frequent mistakes and feelings of deep inadequacy and incompetence.

Children in Matty's situation often become increasingly frustrated and angry. They may give up on trying to please their parents, withdraw into their secret worlds, and opt out of many activities they might have pursued with proper support. Children with support like Ella's, on the other hand, will know that their parents support them—even when they make mistakes or have setbacks. Instead of blaming the child, they will help to find new ways to manage the disability and experience success. And instead of locking themselves in secret worlds, these kids feel comfortable inviting their parents in to communicate and share their lives.

As a parent, I believe the best gift you can give your dyslexic child—in addition to unconditional love, of course—is the gift of understanding. It will be difficult at first for you to put yourself in his shoes (I'll help you do this in greater detail in chapter 5), but in order to reach out to your child and discover his secret life, you must first understand the emotional impact dyslexia has on his daily life.

# 3.
# Us and Them

When the dyslexic boy looks across his classroom and sees the girl who read 20 books over the summer and won the library prize, how do you suppose he feels? When the dyslexic girl is assigned to a team for a project at school and knows her contribution will count for one-quarter of the group's grade, how do you think she feels? Since I'm dyslexic myself, I can tell you: Each feels as if there are two kinds of people in the world—those who are dyslexic (Us) and those who are not (Them).

You've probably felt a sense of Us and Them many times in your life. Perhaps when you were renting and saving for a house, you looked at homeowners as Them. Or if you were an athlete in school, you probably had that feeling as you watched your opponent celebrate after beating your team in a close game. This feeling is common any time you're a little envious of another group and wish you were a part of Them. For most people, these feelings, which are natural, occur only occasionally. For children with dyslexia, Us and

Them is a distinct, ever-present component of their secret life that parents need to understand.

I don't mean to suggest that the dyslexic child views his peers as adversaries; this is not Us *versus* Them. Rather, he simply views the non-dyslexic people he knows as people who will never be afraid to spell a word, to read a passage, or to walk down a hallway and enter the right door to a classroom. The dyslexic child lives with his secret fears in ways that others will never know. He can't help but envy those other kids, to wish that he could be more like them.

# "i'm not like you": two parallel worlds

Let's look more closely at a few areas that make up your child's Us and Them view of the world. Keep in mind that most dyslexic children are of average or above-average intelligence. They may know, on a cognitive level, that others aren't really "smarter" than they. But they may, on an emotional level, feel that they are intellectually impaired—because others are so much more competent and facile than they are. It is almost as if the dyslexic and the non-dyslexic children inhabit two parallel worlds; as children who are growing and learning, they confront the same issues or challenges but in very different ways.

Once a child enters school, he will begin to sense the differences. They may not be apparent to him in kindergarten or first grade, but by second or third grade, he will have a firm sense that he is not quite like other kids. By age 8, I was well aware that I was different, and I had begun to feel isolated and frustrated. Naturally, the awareness is an individual process, with each child sensing his "differentness" on a unique timetable. Mine was a gradual process that began in early childhood and became glaringly obvious by the time I was expected to learn to read. It was clear to me that I was not the same as other children—and I knew I was even different from my parents, neither of whom is dyslexic.

## "I Don't Like to Read"

*Brad often hears his mom say, "It's a great day to curl up on the couch with a good book," but reading is more pain than pleasure for Brad. Curling up with a book has never been a positive experience for him. The letters seem to dance and wiggle on the page. Sometimes, they appear to be superimposed, and he can never understand the main points of a story. For Brad, reading is the worst form of punishment; he'd rather clean both his room and his rabbit's cage than curl up on the couch with a good book. He'd rather shovel heavy snow than read even a comic book.*

For Brad, Us and Them hits hardest when he tries to read. Reading for the dyslexic child is not fun, as it is for so many young readers. When I see a word that I don't know, I unconsciously replace it with another one that's more familiar, without even realizing it. For instance, I might replace "hospice" with "hospital." When my children were old enough to read, I couldn't read them bedtime stories anymore. They knew that I was substituting words that changed the meaning of the story and would stop me in mid-sentence to point out my mistakes. Before they became better readers than I, it was really fun for me to read to them because I made up whatever I wished. Later, they wouldn't so willingly accept my word substitutions.

Often, the dyslexic child may reverse or jumble letters. The word "now" becomes "won." Or the word is simply unintelligible because the letters are so confused. Think of how incredible it would seem for words to actually appear to dance on a page; imagine that you have opened your favorite novel and found that the words are there but some are now in the wrong places.

It's true that not every non-dyslexic child loves to read either. Many kids would rather be outside playing ball, so when it's time to do the required reading, they may resent it. But they don't feel as if their world is ending, as do so many dyslexic children. For example, my son, Kevin, reads for hours on end, but my daughter, A.J., doesn't especially like to read. She's not dyslexic; she just finds reading boring. Her dad finds it downright painful.

## "I Don't Get Good Grades"

*Eva, an 11-year-old, is a bright, hard-working sixth grader. In class, she is full of enthusiasm and ideas. She studies hard and takes her work very seriously. Her friends are always impressed by the way she rambles on about science and history. But when it comes to taking tests, Eva never does very well. She's lucky to get B's, and often she gets only C's. She is very competitive with her classmates and worries constantly about her report card. Her mom tries to downplay the grades, though she always celebrates with a special dinner or a movie when Eva gets a B. But Eva is devastated that she just can't seem to get A's, even in the subjects she loves most.*

For Eva, Us and Them rears its ugly head when she thinks about getting an A. She focuses on the A, or the idea of getting an A, instead of feeling good about herself for trying her best. There are many factors working against the dyslexic child when it comes to school and grades, which I'll discuss in depth in chapter 15. Sometimes, it's the individual teacher's outlook, expectations, or lack of knowledge (or erroneous knowledge) about dyslexia. Some teachers just can't get past the misspelled words or the sloppy handwriting. Thankfully, we now have computers and spell check, but kids who are dyslexic still suffer when there's a test to take.

Non-dyslexic kids may have trouble with grades for various reasons—not enough sleep, a busy schedule, or lack of discipline about studying, for instance—but the dyslexic child's story is quite different. She may work very hard, study overtime, and spend countless hours on homework, only to receive mediocre grades. If the average child put as much effort into studying as many dyslexic kids do, he'd be the class valedictorian. This paradox is difficult for the parent to grasp and certainly feels unfair for the dyslexic child. It isn't easy to watch your child work so hard and receive so few accolades. In chapter 15, we'll talk more about how you can help your child succeed scholastically and feel better about his accomplishments.

## "I Make So Many Mistakes"

*Fifteen-year-old Rory is hoping to attend a private soccer camp, but it is very difficult to get in because so many kids have applied. His coach, Mr. Shroder, has suggested Rory call the camp director and tell him, "Shroder sent me." (Mr. Shroder and the camp director were old college buddies.) Mr. Shroder is confident that Rory would do well. Rory is an articulate, forthright kid with strong soccer skills, but because of his dyslexia, he often mixes up names. When he calls the camp director, Rory freezes and just can't get the word Shroder out. Instead he calls the coach he's known for several years "Mr. Shafer." The camp director is doubtful, and the rest of the conversation seems to go badly. When Rory hangs up, he feels his dream of going to soccer camp is dashed because of that one phone call.*

For Rory, Us and Them just kicked in. The dyslexic child can make mistakes over the most basic things. Certain names and certain words will always get mixed up. A simple word can be misspelled, an obvious fact forgotten. A left turn at the drinking fountain can lead to the girls' room instead of the boys' room (and the picture on the door may not be of any help).

The horror of making a mistake, which every child feels at one time or another, is magnified for the dyslexic child, because the mistake was made over something that to others is simple and basic—something they feel a kindergartner should know. While every child makes mistakes, and generally gets over them, the dyslexic child's recurring embarrassment can keep him from pursuing things he wants to do.

## "I Don't Like Surprises"

*Harry, a middle-school student, is prepared for his history test. He has studied thoroughly and feels confident that he knows all the facts. His teacher has assured the class that it will be a fill-in-the-blanks test, but when Harry arrives at school that day, he overhears the other kids talking excitedly outside the classroom. Mr. Helm has decided to reduce the number of fill-in-the-blank questions in order to add two essay questions that will hold the weight of the grade. Harry knows that no matter what happens now, he will never be able to adjust and prepare in time, even though he has study hall before the exam—which he spends staring at his notes, worrying about the test.*

The idea of Us and Them confronts Harry when he thinks about the fact that Mr. Helm's surprise might just annoy the other kids but inspires panic in him. Dyslexic kids have a particular need for planning ahead; they need to know what's coming up around the corner so they can prepare for it. Surprise quizzes, changes in plans or directions, and last-minute projects can be catastrophic for the dyslexic child. Preparation and organization are key to his success.

Certainly, the non-dyslexic child also does better with structure, limits, and a feeling that his expectations will be met. However, most kids do not get derailed when confronted with a surprise. Most kids will not be happy about the idea of a pop quiz or a last-minute decision to change the instructions on a test, but for the dyslexic child, unexpected changes can determine the difference between success and failure.

## "I Just Don't Fit In"

*Nine-year-old Samantha is at her first sleepover. Her friend Terry has twin 12-year-old sisters, who have also invited a friend to spend the night. Samantha is thrilled to be away from her little brother for an evening and looks forward to a "girls' night out." But when Terry and the other girls suggest they play a game of hearts, she is worried. She wants to play the card game, but the directions sound much too complicated. Luckily, Samantha and her mom have talked about what to do when she isn't comfortable entering an activity or game. "I'll just watch for the first game or two," Samantha says. "Then maybe I'll join in."*

Samantha is steeped in Us and Them at the sleepover. Like most kids, dyslexic children desperately want to fit in, but it's not always easy. In Samantha's case, she wants to fit in with the older girls, but she is confused by the complicated rules of the card game. By watching, dyslexic kids can often figure out what to do, but in social situations with peers, there is often pressure to join right away or to be fast in your thinking. Pressure can make a child with dyslexia hang back or freeze.

Non-dyslexic kids, too, of course, can and do encounter difficulty fitting in, for any number of reasons. Shyness, lack of self-confidence, or physical awkwardness can keep certain kids on the outskirts in social situations. Dyslexic children may have these issues, too, but they also have more difficulty fitting in because many social activities require quick thinking or even verbal wit. The dyslexic child may not get the jokes or readily comprehend subtle verbal cues. As a dyslexic adult, I'm still not immune to this situation. Not wanting to look stupid, I often laugh when I don't understand the joke. When someone says, "I've got a great joke for you!" I cringe inside. Invariably, I will laugh before the punch line; I can tell by the look on the person's face that I've totally missed the point.

## what can parents do?

The emotional and cognitive sides of dyslexia are permanently intertwined. Emotions color every element of the secret life of the dyslexic child. Some experts and learning-disability specialists ignore or miss this point completely. As an educational psychologist, I spend a good deal of time in my sessions with parents of dyslexic children talking about the emotional effects of dyslexia and the many ways parents can help their children counter these effects while fostering confidence and success and minimizing feelings of Us and Them.

Viewing the world as Us and Them causes the child with dyslexia to constantly measure herself against the successes and triumphs of others, instead of establishing her own personal best. I encourage parents to remember that helping their child to learn to do her best—and accepting and celebrating her best, without comparing herself to others—is an important component of my program. Helping her understand that she is not "dumb" but merely has a learning problem is a step in the right direction. Still, it is hard to explain this to a child who just wants to be like everyone else. As a parent, you must reach across the emotional chasm to connect with and reassure your dyslexic child. She will probably always feel some sense of "Us and Them" due to her disability, but by encouraging her to reach her own potential, you will help her focus more on her strengths and less on how she compares with others.

For many parents, understanding the concept of Us and Them is the portal through which they understand the secret life of their dyslexic child. Once you understand that there will always be Thems in your child's life—the kids who get great grades without studying, the kids who zip through their homework, and so on—you can work to normalize the balance. Life for your child must not become a competition between two teams. In chapter 6, I'll talk more about specific ways to help bridge the gap between Us and Them.

Normalizing means reassuring your child on a consistent basis that everyone has things that he's good at and things that are hard for him. Anne Marie, for instance, might read out loud and sound like a professional actress, but your child may be very artistic or very creative at designing spaceships in his mind and building them with his K'nex or Lego set with no help at all. Jonathan, the kid next door, might enjoy writing stories on the computer, but your child may be the fastest runner on the track team or have such a sweet disposition that other kids love to play with him. It can be very helpful to tell your child what your own struggles are and that there are things that are always a challenge for you, so he knows that strengths and weaknesses are a part of every person's daily life.

Learning not to be competitive is a lifelong struggle for everyone, certainly. But once you understand the concept of Us and Them, then the importance of helping your child discover, foster, and appreciate his strengths becomes crystal clear. Your child needs to learn that the tasks that are hard for him don't "define" him, that doing his best is good enough. Most parents brag about what their kids are good at to others but rarely to the child himself. Tell your child, too. Kids can't read minds, just like you can't. This reassurance should be cumulative—if it's consistently a part of your support, it will go a long way in helping your child tackle and get through those more challenging tasks.

# 4. Why Can't I Be Like Everyone Else?

**Peter gasps when he gets his history test back.** He had studied for 4 hours and still only got a C. Ryan, who sits next to him, proudly displays his A. Ryan boasts that he studied for 45 minutes and also went to a movie last night. Peter wonders why things come so easily for other kids. Why can't he be like everyone else? To make matters worse, the teacher has let the kids correct the test in class. Peter is embarrassed that Ryan has seen all his mistakes. He couldn't remember how to spell several presidents' names in the fill-in-the-blank section, and he has gotten basic dates mixed up, too.

## how it feels to be different

A child with dyslexia experiences its effects 24/7, all day every day. It's a lifelong issue for each child. Kids who have dyslexia often ask, "Why can't I be normal? Why does this always happen to me?" Even when they're old enough to understand their problem and to utilize coping strategies, it is still difficult not to feel inferior to or "different" from others who seem to accomplish things so easily.

While he may appear happy and well-adjusted, it's quite likely that the dyslexic child has many questions about why he's not more like his peers. He doesn't want to hide in fear of his disability. He doesn't want to pretend. He doesn't want to "have strategies." And even though he doesn't know this himself at a young age, he wants his parents—and everyone in his world—to know that his dyslexia is real, and it's not just going to go away. It's an element of his existence; it's a distinct, real part of him. In the dyslexic children I have worked with, it is when a child's parents understand what he encounters in his everyday life, his secret life, that the child perceives his learning disability with a more positive attitude and it doesn't seem so daunting or overwhelming. And when a parent can think outside the box, outside his or her own everyday perceptions, that's when real progress and success happen.

Imagine how frustrating it must be to watch out the window while other kids are playing ball and your homework takes you two or three times longer to complete than does everyone else's. Or how difficult it is to search your memory for an answer only to find it long after all the other hands in the class have gone up. Or to struggle with a reading assignment only to discover that you've missed the crucial point of the story. There is no doubt that the dyslexic child approaches life from a perspective that others can only imagine. Let's take a look at some of the feelings your child may be experiencing.

## "I Feel Inferior"

*Shirleen is the eldest of three sisters. Her younger sisters, who are 11 and 13, are very sharp-witted. On the way to the beach each weekend, they love to play brainteaser games in the car. Their dad, who is a sociology pro-*

*fessor, encourages and participates in the intellectual dueling, and the level of their banter is quite advanced as her sisters and dad challenge one another. Shirleen always sits in the back of the van, listening to music on her headphones. Her brain just doesn't work fast enough to answer the questions. By the time she's figured out what the question is, one of her little sisters already has the answer. Shirleen loves her family, but she can't help feeling inferior to Ava and Grace, even though they are younger than she.*

It's natural for kids to experience feelings of inferiority. How can a dyslexic child avoid it, when other kids seem to do things so easily and so much better? In our competitive world, the child who is fastest and brightest usually grabs the brass ring before the dyslexic child has even boarded the carousel. It's especially difficult when a younger sibling seems to have all the answers or when a best friend aces every test.

I encourage you to take the competition out of the learning process or your dyslexic child may always feel intellectually inferior. Encourage your child to think of her own strengths, rather than dwell enviously on the strengths of others. Perhaps your child's sibling is a great reader, but your child may have a real flair for ice-skating or math. Remind her consistently that all people have strengths and weaknesses, whether they are dyslexic or not. (Tell her about your own.) Learning should not be about competition; the current sensibilities toward that kind of thinking are especially detrimental to kids with learning disabilities.

## "I Feel Angry"

*Sam, a dyslexic fourth grader, has been in five fights in as many weeks. He is an angry boy with curly black hair and freckles who can fly off the handle at the slightest provocation. Although he is a class clown and is well-liked by his peers and teachers, his short fuse often lands him in trouble. When the principal calls him to his office, Sam is defensive. "It's all their fault," he accuses. He is unwilling to take responsibility for his own aggressive behavior, but the principal can't be fooled.*

I was a lot like Sam when I was a kid. I had a great deal of pent-up anger as a result of my dyslexia, and I often wound up in fights in the school yard. Fortunately, I found an outlet for my energy—I became an excellent runner and channeled my anger into a positive activity. It's important to help your child find an outlet for his anger. Very often for a dyslexic child, a sport that allows him to burn off some energy and enjoy feelings of excelling is ideal.

Anger is a predictable reaction to dyslexia. Talking about anger with your child helps a great deal; let him know it's okay to be angry but not okay to hurt others or break things. Make a conscious effort to sit down with your child and discuss his feelings about his disability. Pretending those feelings aren't there won't make them go away. Knowing that he can talk to you about his feelings of anger and that you won't shame or ridicule him helps your child tremendously. It's important to tell your child often, "I'm here to help. I understand how you might feel."

## "I Feel Jealous"

*Rebecca and Stephanie are best friends in the same class at school. Although Rebecca considers Stephanie to be the nicest girl she's ever met, she harbors a secret resentment toward her. It just doesn't seem fair that Stephanie gets A's without studying and that she is such a terrific poet. In fifth grade, Stephanie actually wrote, illustrated, and self-produced her own picture book on her computer, and it's on display in the school library. Rebecca detests writing and wasn't invited to join the poetry club Stephanie started after school. Rebecca hates feeling so envious of her best friend, but she just can't help it.*

Your dyslexic child is bound to feel jealous of other kids at times. She'll wonder why it takes her two hours to write the same paragraph that it takes her friend 15 minutes. She'll be sitting at the dining room table, poring over her studies, while she knows that the other kids from her class are already chatting on the computer. She'll wonder why she has to shoulder this burden when her kid sister can read Harry Potter over a weekend.

To help counter feelings of jealousy, help your child focus on what she does best and maintain a positive attitude. Rebecca's mom and dad can remind her that Stephanie may very well be a great poet, but there's no one with a voice as sweet as Rebecca's or such a great soccer kick. Encourage your child to focus on her own development and progress without comparing herself with her peers or siblings. This doesn't mean allowing her to abandon her scholastic work; it just means pointing out that some things will come very easily to her, and other things will be more difficult to master.

## "I Feel Embarrassed"

*Susan, a middle-school student, has run to the corner store for some ice cream and cones. She chooses the ice cream her little brother likes; she doesn't know the name, but she recognizes the colorful design on the label. Susan often uses visualization to distinguish products. On her way to the checkout counter, she literally bumps into Danik, a really cool girl in her class. "Wow!" Danik says, "that looks like a yummy flavor. What's it called?" Susan is tongue-tied and blushing; she can't remember the name, and she isn't sure if she can read it correctly, either. She certainly doesn't want to try in front of Danik. Instead, she holds up the box so Danik can see the label. "Oh! Confetti! Sounds good."*

Dyslexia can cause a great deal of embarrassment, but as your child grows older and learns, with your help, to become more honest about her problem, she will discover that embarrassment isn't the worst thing in the world. In chapter 6, I'll talk about how to bridge the gap between Us and Them and how you can help your child learn to laugh at herself and to feel comfortable revealing rather than hiding her disability. The dyslexic child's tendency to retreat into secrecy and shame makes the embarrassment all the worse.

## "I Feel Alone"

*Juan, a 12-year-old, is listening to the kids talk about a story they have read at home for CCD, a religious class, which meets in the church on Thursdays after school. He tries to join in the conversation, but each time he makes an observation, the other students seem to ignore him. He's beginning to wonder if he has even read the right story, since it seems that he has gotten something totally different out of the assignment than the other kids. Mrs. Hunkins, who leads the group, is nice enough, but she, too, doesn't appear to be very interested in what Juan has to say. He sits silently at the table, listening as the other kids share their ideas, wondering why he didn't pick up on any of this when he was reading. He feels so alone.*

Juan feels as if he is the only one in the class who hasn't understood the reading assignment. He thought he'd picked up on the main points, but apparently not. When his peers can do something, especially something as basic and vital as reading and comprehending, the dyslexic child can feel truly alone, as if no one in the world has a similar problem. Imagine how you might feel if you accompanied your spouse to a college or high-school reunion, and all the former students were laughing about past experiences and sharing private jokes that you didn't get. That's a bit what it feels like to be dyslexic in a world where everyone else can read, write, and spell. It's a solitary feeling to be in a room full of individuals who are rapidly exchanging ideas and sharing experiences and not be able to comprehend readily or connect to what they are saying. The dyslexic child feels that he is the only one in the world who doesn't "get it."

# helping your child handle his emotions

What can you do to help your child deal with these disturbing feelings? I'll talk about specific strategies in later chapters, but for now, the most important thing to remember is to be supportive and let your child know it's okay to have and to talk about his feelings. As a parent, you need to understand that your child will experience these emotions. Sometimes, he will feel angry, alone, frustrated, or defeated. Be patient and offer support. But also remind your child that there are many other dyslexic children in the world. He is not really alone; sometimes, it just feels that way.

Sometimes, you will need to sit with your child and discuss these issues; at other times, it's best to take a break. Go to a movie, shoot some hoops, take a walk together. Try to help your child focus on the positive aspects of his life and steer him toward the activities that give him pleasure. As with any disability, be sensitive to the fact that there are times to confront it head-on and times to focus on other issues and pastimes.

The best way to support your dyslexic child is to be there for him and to be patient with his feelings. Denying that your child will sometimes experience these emotions or telling him not to feel that way isn't productive. Let your child know that it's okay to feel as he does, but always assure him you will help him find ways to manage his dyslexia.

getting inside

your child's

secret life

# part 2

# 5. Think like Your Child

**As a parent,** you can know every strategy in the world to help your dyslexic child (and you'll learn some terrific ones in parts 3 and 4), but if you can't think like your child, I'm convinced those strategies won't really work. You need to get inside your child's head and understand what it's like to be him. You need to know that there are some words—even easy words—he will always have difficulty getting right and that there are certain times of the day when he will always have trouble following directions properly or remembering certain facts. If you ignore these realities, you will simply be a drillmaster, with little understanding of the emotions and frustrations that your child experiences on a daily, ongoing basis.

## take a walk in your child's shoes

Here are some exercises you can use to help understand what life looks like—and even more importantly, *feels* like—from your dyslexic child's perspective. Some of these might make you so uncomfortable that you won't even want to try them—and I don't blame you. Read them over, though, and imagine what it might be like to walk in your child's shoes every day. Even if your child's own form of dyslexia doesn't affect her in each and every one of these categories of exercises, it's likely she has done things exactly like these examples and knows what it feels like to go through experiences like these. Now, you will, too.

## Challenges with Processing Language

Of all the challenges people with dyslexia face, problems processing language—including spelling and writing—are the most commonly recognized ones. However, few people without dyslexia understand the complexities of this problem and the frustrations it can cause in both the classroom and the everyday world.

**Limit your letters.** Try to carry on a conversation while leaving out words that contain one or two letters of the alphabet. For example, try to speak without using words that contain "f" or "t." You'll find yourself having to substitute words or phrases that have similar meanings but don't say exactly the same thing. You'll no doubt end up speaking in a very roundabout way. See if you can keep this up for a 10-minute conversation. How long does it take for the person you're speaking with to notice something is different in the way you're talking?

Oftentimes, dyslexics have difficulty processing words. This exercise shows you how it feels to have to think about every word you say and how it feels to be slowed down while speaking. This is how a dyslexic child may feel when reading or trying to recall something from memory. As she processes information, her speaking and reading skills may come to a crawl. As you search your brain to come up with words that don't include an "f," a "t," or another letter of your choice, you will experience the same sense of frustration and hard work that your child feels when she is searching for words to say, read, or write. Remember, this isn't just a 10-minute exercise for your child; it's an all-day, every-day challenge.

**Find the proper spelling of a name.** To understand the complications not being able to spell easily can cause, pretend that you can't spell a common name, such as Robert or Elizabeth. Now, figure out a way to find that name printed somewhere so you can see exactly how it's spelled. Proper names aren't in the dictionary. You can try a phone book, but remember, first names are often abbreviated there. Maybe you can find some other kind of directory or find someone with that name in an encyclopedia. Keep looking until you locate the name. Make note of the time you spend on this activity. Now try it for a more unusual first name, like Miriam or Selene.

You may be surprised at how long it takes you to confirm the spelling of a common name. As you searched for the name, did you feel anxious or frustrated? Imagine that there's a time limit on your search: You need to get the name on an envelope within 5 minutes, when the postman is due to pick up. Or imagine that a client is waiting for you to deliver a report with his name properly spelled on the cover. For a child with dyslexia, such seemingly simple tasks can become a lengthy, cumbersome process.

**Live in a pressure cooker.** Imagine you have just sat down in the first row of a packed auditorium to enjoy a play. Three minutes before curtain time, an usher approaches you and asks you to read some announcements to the crowd because the regular announcer has taken ill. When you look at the announcements, you see they're in very small print, filled with unfamiliar foreign names and composed in long, complicated sentences that make the writing seem like some kind of legal document. Everyone in the theater is staring at you as you walk up to the microphone.

Though you probably won't ever actually get put on the spot like this, thinking about what it might be like will give you a sense of what your dyslexic child experiences when he's asked to read in public. The amount of stress and tension that you might feel performing in front of a live audience without preparation is similar to what your dyslexic child experiences each time he has to read a paragraph—or maybe even a single word or name—in front of his peers.

**Take Foreign Language 101.** Visit a classroom, seminar, or religious service—or even watch an hour-long television show or video—conducted in a language that is foreign to you. If you are English speaking, for instance, sit in on a Spanish-speaking group or show. Then try to describe exactly what took place.

For kids with severe dyslexia, trying to follow a classroom discussion can be similar to listening to a foreign language. As a result, they may rely on other senses to help them figure out what's going on, because not every word is clear or comprehensible.

During the exercise, you probably watched for nonverbal cues to help you discern what was taking place. If you chose a classroom, could you tell when it was recess time just by looking at the children's faces? If you attended a seminar or worship service, did the body language of the attendees give you hints about which parts were most interesting and important to them? Could you tell the emotions of the people on the TV show just by their tone of voice? Did you begin to tune out some of the words as you zeroed in on these nonverbal cues?

As the words blur by him, a dyslexic child often finds himself concentrating on nonverbal cues. By doing this, he may be able to piece together the gist of what's going on, but he won't be able to completely fathom the subtleties of the situation that are being communicated through spoken language.

**Switch hands.** To understand the frustrations your child might be feeling when he tries to write, spend a day writing everything with your opposite hand.

Be sure to note the reactions of your spouse, colleagues, and peers when you write with your nondominant hand. Does anyone comment on your sloppy handwriting or look askance at you because it appears so childlike? Many dyslexic children have sloppy handwriting. How do you feel when others react to your awkward scrawl? Does it take you a lot longer to write? This is just a regular day for many dyslexic children.

## Challenges with Numbers

Dealing with numbers can present problems for your child even when he's far away from algebra class. Tasks that others take for granted, such as recalling the series of numbers in a zip code or telephone number, can prove particularly challenging for a child with dyslexia. The following exercises will help you to understand how simply transposing some numbers can have drastic results.

**Find an address.** Choose a street that's close to home but that you don't usually travel. Now drive up and down the street, looking for house number 17. Then enter a municipal building or public office complex and look for room 232.

We've all struggled at times to follow a map or sort out the directions to a friend's house. But in this exercise, you experienced what it feels like to search for a location that you're not even sure exists. Did you feel disoriented, frustrated, or confused? Did you ask for help? If so, you might have been greeted with some strange looks if the address doesn't exist. This experience happens frequently to dyslexic children. They may be totally convinced that they will find a store or their friend's house or a classroom that they've been assigned to, but they can't because they've copied down the address wrong.

**Dial a wrong number.** To experience the embarrassment and frustration of making the same error repeatedly, pick a telephone number that you call frequently and then transpose two of the digits. Dial the number and then quickly apologize to the person who answers. Then dial the same number again. Note the person's attitude when you explain that you misdialed for a second time. Finally, reverse two other digits and repeat. Apologize each time you make a mistake.

Simply dialing a telephone number can be a frustrating task for dyslexics. And quite often, kids who reverse numbers make the same mistakes over and over again. What was the reaction of the person on the other end of the line? Angry? Annoyed? Even if he was polite, how many more times do you think you could call that number before the person became aggravated with you?

**Check your check-writing ability.** Write out a check to yourself for a large amount, such as $836.68, but spell the number wrong, such as six hundred sixty-eight dollars and 83 cents. Then go to your bank and try to cash the check. After the initial confusion and discussion over what the right number is, ask the teller to spell the numbers properly for you.

How does the teller react when she sees the discrepancy? Does her reaction make you feel a little stupid? Or worse, did she treat you like some kind of criminal? The irony of the situation isn't lost on a person with dyslexia: It's your check and you have money in the bank, but the bank won't cash it for you until you can get that number right!

**Try to be letter perfect.** Address an envelope but transpose some numbers in the street address and put the wrong zip code on it. Mail the letter and wait to see what happens. (Put an accurate return address on the letter.)

Take a guess—what do you think will happen? Well, it may actually arrive safely, or it may show up at your return address several weeks from now—or it may never be seen again! Imagine if you felt that way about every letter you addressed. What if the letter was important, and you really wanted the person to get it on time? Do you think you'd be frustrated by (and worried about) the amount of time you have to wait just to see if the letter has arrived?

**Doctor that form.** Visit a new doctor and fill in incorrect numbers on the medical form. Think about what you will say when the nurse notices that you are clearly not 615 pounds or could not have been born in 1995. If she doesn't notice right away, let her know you may have made some mistakes on the form and ask if she can help you correct them.

Unless you have dyslexia, you've probably never thought about the numerous forms, surveys, and other documents that require you to record numbers. A standard medical form that requires you to record your weight and date of birth can present a real challenge to someone with dyslexia. Imagine you are your child being asked to fill out a simple form in school. Do you think she experiences the same sense of frustration or embarrassment you felt?

## Challenges with Processing Information

Has your dyslexic child ever been accused of not paying attention? By trying out the exercises below, you'll get a better understanding of why your child may have problems following directions or understanding what he reads.

**Get hit with a double whammy.** Find a news station on the radio. Now turn on the television and tune in to the Weather Channel or an all-news station. Listen to both simultaneously for 10 minutes. Then try to recount the details of both programs.

This exercise recreates the experience of information overload that is common with dyslexia. When a dyslexic person hears a long list of items or directions to follow, the information may become jumbled in his mind. When you were bombarded with both images on the TV screen and chatter from the radio, did you feel unable to concentrate on either one? Do you feel confident that you understand what was reported from either source? Probably not. Likewise, when your child is given a number of directives at once, he may feel that his brain is being overloaded and that there are just too many facts for him to remember. What may appear to be hesitation on your child's part to follow through on the directives may simply be his attempt to sort out the information in his mind.

**Miss the message.** Pick up a novel and read a chapter from the middle of the book. Then write a paragraph about what you've read, highlighting only the most minor details and ignoring the main elements of the plot. Include only extraneous facts or descriptions.

When doing this exercise, you'll notice two things. First, because you didn't read the earlier chapters, you're going to have trouble following the story: who the characters are, why they are doing what they're doing, and what exactly is important. You're probably not going to be able to give a meaningful account of what's going on. Second, when you focus only on descriptions and minor developments in the story, you can tell that nobody is going to derive much use from your paragraph.

Often, dyslexic kids miss the main points of stories or books they have read. Consider what it must feel like to be the only person in a class or group to not understand the basics of something you have all just read. Likewise, imagine how difficult it must be to study and understand information in a textbook when you are unable to identify main themes and points. When you take these feelings into account, it's easy to understand why reading is often not a pleasurable experience for people with dyslexia.

**Get on the same page.** After your spouse or friend has read a newspaper or magazine story, pick up the same article and read through it. Then discuss the article but change some of the important facts in the story. (For example, if the story is about an actor who just won an Oscar, talk about the article as if it were about the actor announcing he was getting divorced or as if it were about a completely different actor winning the award.) Watch for the other person's reaction when you distort and confuse the details.

Dyslexic kids often have trouble getting the facts straight after they've read a passage. How does it feel for you, as an adult, to jumble up the facts? Are others patient with you as you present erroneous information, or do they become impatient or upset? Stick to your guns and say how sure you are that you've got it right. How do you begin to feel as others refute your rendition of the news story?

**Reach for the wrong word.** When riding in a car with a group of adults, read a sign aloud but change one of the words or numbers. Watch for everyone's reaction.

Whether you've said turn right instead of left, misread the name of a local restaurant (Flappers instead of Slappers), or told them the speed limit was 25 instead of 55, most likely your friends will jump down your throat and point out your mistake.

Dyslexic children make lots of mistakes when reading, and they may be constantly getting corrected by their peers or adults outside the home. Sometimes, dealing with the scorn of others when you make a mistake is much worse than the actual effects of the error, such as winding up on the wrong road or misinterpreting a billboard. How would you feel if this happened to you a couple times a day? Would you read aloud less frequently? Would you be waiting in fear to see if what you said was actually right every time you read something to someone else?

**Write a paragraph.** Without any preparation, sit down and write a paragraph explaining how to disassemble and reassemble your garage door. Do not consult any kind of manual or reference book that would explain the task.

This exercise is actually the opposite of what a dyslexic child would do, but the result is the same: confusion over how to organize your thoughts. He may sit for an hour preparing elaborate notes, only to find that when he begins his paragraph, his thoughts are completely disorganized, as if he hadn't prepared anything at all. In this example, he may be able to tell you all the parts of the garage door but not be able to recall all their names, explain the process, or list the tools you'd use to take the door down and put it back up again. Imagine how difficult it is to explain a complicated process without being able to map out the parts of your paragraph beforehand. The dyslexic child may be confused about where to begin, what the major elements of the paragraph should be, which essential parts he should convey, and what order everything should be in.

## Challenges with Spatial Skills and Chronology

Like words and numbers, directions such as right or left and north or south can become confused in a dyslexic person's brain. Similarly, a person with dyslexia may have trouble organizing items, such as creating a filing system or grasping the concept of chronology. The following activities will help you better understand the frustrations these challenges can cause.

**Take the opposite tack.** Take a walk to a familiar place in your neighborhood. Once you arrive at the destination, stop and try to recall every intersection you passed on your way there. Make a mental list of whether you went left, right, or straight. Now try to get yourself home. However, when you get to the first intersection on your return trip, rather than automatically turning the proper way, flip a coin and turn right for heads, left for tails. At the second intersection, turn the proper way to get yourself toward home, but then continue to alternate every other intersection between flipping the coin to determine which way to turn and proceeding the way you know is correct. Continue doing this for 20 minutes, or until you get home.

Feeling frustrated yet? Note how long it took you to get home—if you even made it there under the 30-minute deadline. This exercise recreates the sense of concentration required of a dyslexic child when he's told to go left or right. Rather than intuitively knowing which way to turn, a person with dyslexia must be conscious of each direction she takes, since she can't rely on automatically turning in the proper direction.

**File your failure.** Make photocopies of some important papers. Look for an obscure word on one of the pages and file the papers under that word, in an area that has no relation to the label on the file. Wait several weeks and then try to find them. Alternatively, try to find a paid bill or bank account balance in your files that includes the number $34.95.

Are you having trouble locating those papers that you misfiled? How did you go about finding a bill with that number on it? You certainly didn't file it that way, so it must have taken some serious thought—and probably quite a lot of trial and error. Not only does your dyslexic child have difficulty retrieving information he has filed in his brain, but he may also have difficulty with organizational skills such as properly recording and organizing information in notebooks and folders. Note the amount of extra time it took to locate the papers. How much worse would you feel if someone were waiting on the phone to discuss the paperwork or if finding those papers were critical to paying a bill on time?

**Create chronology chaos.** Record your morning routine on index cards, with one task per card. For example, each card might have one of the following tasks on it: turn off the alarm, put on robe and slippers, let the dog out, eat breakfast, brush teeth, shower, dress, fix hair, and grab keys. Now shuffle the index cards. Do your best to remember the new order of the tasks. Tomorrow morning, do the tasks in this new sequence.

How did it feel to be unsure of what you should be doing next? No doubt this new sequence left you feeling out of sorts. Perhaps you had to brush your teeth before eating breakfast. Maybe you got dressed and then realized you hadn't yet showered. Did this mixed-up routine leave you feeling less than ready to start the new day? Did you leave the house with the nagging feeling that you may have forgotten to do something? Most of us take our routines for granted, but for the dyslexic person, not knowing what step comes next in a sequence is a common experience.

## Challenges with the Reactions of Others

Especially if they need to complete a task quickly, children with dyslexia may need to ask for help. But since dyslexia can't be seen, the kids' questions are often met with confusion, exasperation, or even anger. To an outsider, the answer to the question may seem obvious—yet it is anything but obvious to a dyslexic child. If you're feeling brave, try a few of the following exercises and note the reactions you get.

**Annoy someone.** Go up to someone you know will be very annoyed (perhaps a very busy clerk in a store or a bouncer at a nightclub) and ask him to help you with a trivial problem like tying your shoe or reading a simple map.

Though this exercise may not be pleasant, you'll get to see how people react when they think you're wasting their time. How do you feel about yourself when someone barks at you or gives you dirty looks? Often, people will yell even louder if you don't seem to understand what they're saying, as if the volume of their answer will somehow make everything clear.

As a parent, you might encourage your child to "speak up" when he needs help. After doing this exercise, though, it's easy to see that he may stop asking for help if he's given grief or made to feel inferior. Of course, by not asking for help, he will just fall farther and farther behind his peers, creating a vicious circle of frustration.

**Play lawyer.** Imagine you've been asked to serve as a lawyer representing a client in small-claims court. Do you know the protocol? How will you address the judge when you arrive in the court? Imagine how the judge is reacting as you argue your case.

Chances are, even though you've seen cases on TV, you won't know exactly how a lawyer proceeds in small-claims court. Do you think the judge would look kindly upon your lack of proper knowledge and protocol? Does your lack of knowledge mean that you are not intelligent or merely that you're unprepared? Your dyslexic child probably knows what this feels like. Often, other people expect her to do something that she just doesn't quite know how to do. It may seem to others (or, sadly, to your child herself) that she's not smart enough to know what to do—when really it's just that she's caught off guard.

**Spell it again, Sam.** Ask a colleague or a librarian to spell a list of simple names and words for you, like William, Arthur, Rebecca, apple, type, and world. When they hesitate, tell them you are dyslexic and note their reaction.

If you're lucky, the person you approach will happily spell the words. More likely, however, your colleague will give you a strange look and show signs of being uncomfortable—or will laugh as if you're making a joke. People often don't know how to respond to dyslexia; some may become irritated, embarrassed, or convinced you are kidding. Think about how various people respond to your child's dyslexia on a daily basis.

**Be in the wrong place.** Next time you go out to dinner at a fancy restaurant, knock on the bathroom door of the opposite gender, poke your head in, and ask if this is the right room.

How embarrassing! Can't you see the sign on the door? Apparently not, especially if you are dyslexic. You might have been confused by the French words, by the font of the lettering, or by the odd little pictures on the doors. Whatever your excuse, you've ended up in the wrong place at the wrong time, a common experience for many dyslexics.

# the bottom line

What do I hope you've gained from these exercises? A better understanding of what it means to be dyslexic and a better grasp of the emotions your child is experiencing every day of his life. I imagine you may have been too embarrassed to actually carry out some of these exercises. But remember, your dyslexic child doesn't have the luxury of choice. He goes through events like these every day, whether he wants to or not. Perhaps what is most valuable about these exercises, then, is your deepening understanding of how challenging these puzzles are to your child. When confronted with these exercises, you may well be tempted to just give up. Giving up is not an option for your child.

# 6. Bridging the Gap between Us and Them

**Even though your child** will always feel a sense of "Us and Them," you can help him find ways to live comfortably and successfully among others. In this chapter, I'll give you practical strategies for helping your child not only survive but thrive.

## a secret he shouldn't keep

One of the most important things you can do is to help your child find ways to tell others about his dyslexia. When I make a call to someone who quickly rattles off a name or a series of facts she expects me to scribble down, I need to stop, tell her that I am dyslexic, and ask her to spell or repeat the information slowly. But often, people laugh or get annoyed; this is an area in which the gap between Us and Them is readily apparent.

The best way to handle this problem is to explain clearly but succinctly what dyslexia is and what it entails. For instance, at the beginning of a conversation, I often say, "You may have to speak slowly or write things down for me now and then because I'm dyslexic. This means I have difficulty processing and writing information." This gives people pause to think. "Oh!" they may respond. "I've heard of that. Tell me more about it."

You can teach your child a simple phrase to use as well. Setting your child up with an uncomplicated explanation of his disability will help him as he encounters new people and situations. You could, for instance, teach your child to say "I have a learning disability. That means I have trouble spelling and reading" or "I have a learning problem so I need extra help with spelling and listening." Use simple words to describe how your child's dyslexia most commonly manifests itself. This will help others better understand and aid him. Giving your child words he can grasp will also help him feel more at ease with his unique style of learning.

# ways to bridge the gap

Although you are aware that your child keenly feels the differences between herself and non-dyslexics on a daily basis, you can help her by reminding her of the many ways in which all people are the same. In addition to helping her feel comfortable revealing her dyslexia, you can also help by reinforcing the following concepts and strategies.

**Help her seek and find others who best understand her.** When any child encounters a playmate who constantly teases, parents often find it helpful to remind her that there are other kids with whom she can choose to play. The same is true of dyslexic children. They may need to be reminded that there are plenty of children and adults who understand them and will be supportive, friendly, and helpful. I often gravitate toward people who gently correct my mistakes or who know me so well that they'll actually finish my sentences for me if I'm having a bad day. Help your child make a list of those people (children and adults) and help fashion your child's schedule so she spends time regularly with them. Revisit and update the list several times a year.

**Limit problem situations and be prepared.** Although your child must live in a world with others, you may be able to limit the situations that you know will cause her great difficulty. This may seem obvious, but parents who don't "think like their child" often unknowingly contribute to problems by allowing their children to be placed in uncomfortable situations, such as reading aloud or being expected to follow complicated directions.

Of course, difficult situations can't—and shouldn't—always be avoided. When you know your child will be facing a challenging situation, help her to prepare and rehearse. For example, if you know she will be asked to fill out a form when she applies for a school club or activity, inquire ahead of time if she can bring the form home and return it the next day (I use this same method when I need to bring a form to my doctor's office).

**Help him help others.** We each have something to offer others. One of the keys to bridging the gap between Us and Them is to understand that every individual has both strengths that can be summoned as well as weaknesses. Help your child develop the confidence to communicate his own strengths and weaknesses to others and to be aware of theirs.

**Smile.** A healthy sense of humor is one of the best ways to bridge the gap. Help your child keep a lighter perspective on his mistakes and put others at ease. This shouldn't undermine the seriousness of the task at hand, but if, for instance, your 10-year-old makes a wrong turn in a familiar hallway, you can remind him, "Oh! There's that confusing corner playing tricks with me again! Remember to think about left and right before you turn!"

I often give my students open-book exams. Some days, I have real difficulty reading the questions aloud. When that happens, I ask my students to pitch in and help by pronouncing words that are causing me trouble. I try to have fun with the situation and turn the quiz into a sort of game involving the students (who find me quite amusing at times).

**Find an outlet for success.** Others will admire your child for what she does well, once you help her find an outlet for success. Whether it's swimming, artwork, or being a good friend—find your child's gifts and help her to pursue them and enjoy the sense of confidence and accomplishment they bring. Give her plenty of opportunity to try new activities until she finds an area that motivates her.

**Prepare her for when people aren't nice.** Let your child know that there will always be some people in the world who won't understand her and may not be nice. This is a tough lesson that all kids need to learn. Help her understand that this should not stand in her way. Let her know that some people make fun of others for all kinds of reasons and that kids without learning disabilities get teased, too. Talk about why others might tease or be rude. Does that person have insecurities or problems of his own? If you instill a sense of belief in herself, your child will be able to withstand insults and know that she is strong and capable. Also remind her that just because some kids tease her about her reading, it's no reason to turn around and tease others about their clothes or looks or other things. Help her break out of this vicious cycle.

**Give your child manageable responsibilities.** At home, give your child tasks that he will handle well. For instance, let him empty the dishwasher or feed the hamster; but don't expect him to keep track of the family calendar or organize his desk. Involve your child in the decision. Having control over his actions enhances his self-esteem. To feel that he's an important part of the family, he needs to experience both the respect and the sense of responsibility that his non-dyslexic siblings feel.

**Take the time to be with your child.** Relationships are built by being there. My mom spent hours with me, helping me negotiate schoolwork and supporting me emotionally as I learned to deal with my dyslexia. Today, we still have a strong, mutually supportive relationship. Your child may not always appreciate the hours you put in now, but as she grows older, the time you give to her will form the foundation of a strong, loving relationship.

**Talk with teachers.** An important way to help your child bridge the gap is to keep communications wide open with his teachers. We'll talk more about this in chapter 15.

# life lessons that bring two worlds together

As you work to help your child bridge the gap between Us and Them, you will encounter a variety of situations in which your support and input will make a crucial difference. Here are some of the most important life lessons you should teach your child. These are simple but powerful ways in which you can play a vital role in your child's success now and long into adulthood.

## You Don't Have to Fear Reading

*Arleen, an 11-year-old dyslexic, is one of five children in her school who have won an essay contest about what they love about their town. Arleen worked on the essay for weeks, and her mom helped her type it into the computer so it would look neat. Arleen is thrilled that she's been selected as a winner, but now she's expected to read her essay aloud at a school assembly. She is terrified. She's proud that she won but can't bear the thought of making a fool of herself in front of her classmates.*

Just as Arleen's mom helped her prepare (but not actually write) her essay, she can also help her prepare for reading aloud. There are very few dyslexic individuals who will ever be completely comfortable reading aloud. But since Arleen is proud of her essay and her accomplishment, she should be encouraged to "go for it." The key is preparing her in advance so that she will be able to succeed.

One tactic to help prepare for reading aloud that I find works quite well is to allow the child to write the passage out, breaking down difficult or troublesome words into segments. For example, if your child has difficulty pronouncing or reading the word *acrobat*, let her segment the word so it makes sense to her when reading. Although the dictionary instructs us to break the word *a-cro-bat*, your dyslexic child may find that she reads and understands the word better when she writes the word out like this: *ac-rob-at*. There is no hard and fast rule for how a dyslexic best understands a word, so the segmentation should be left to the child. The point of this exercise is to help your child read aloud, not to teach by the dictionary.

Using this method, Arleen can retype or rewrite her essay, segmenting the words so that she will be able to read them more fluently. In addition, she should practice at home in advance of the assembly. Arranging for a supportive teacher to stand nearby during the children's presentations means someone will be there to offer help if Arleen stumbles. In a classroom situation, you can ensure that your dyslexic child is given this same kind of support and time to prepare by talking to the teacher and making sure he understands your child's particular needs.

Although Arleen may feel uncomfortable about the extra preparation required for her to read her piece aloud, she will also appreciate the support from her parents and teacher. By preparing your child to read aloud, you contribute to her sense of confidence and let her know that although she may need special help in this area, she can face this challenge and she can succeed. It is important to help your dyslexic child understand that it is okay to seek help and that she does not have to go through life trying to avoid difficult situations.

## Learning Is More Than Getting Good Grades

*Kevin is determined to get an A in English, even though reading and writing are very difficult for him. For the first exam of the year, he studies for more than six hours and seems to know all the material. Though he does very well on the multiple-choice questions, he falters with the essay, even though special accommodations have been made for him because of his dyslexia. When he comes home with a B on the test, he slams his books on the kitchen counter and stomps up to his room. His parents, who are proud of Kevin's efforts and achievements, know that they will have a hard time convincing him that a B still means he did a great job.*

The best way to deal with academic competitiveness is to counteract it with your own family's outlook on the value of learning. If you raise your child to believe that he must get A's and be first in every contest, he is naturally going to be hard on himself. But if you give him the message that what is most important is learning—not getting A's—then his focus will be on his individual growth, not academic achievement. This message is particularly important for the dyslexic child.

The fact is, when your child gets his first job, chances are no one is going to ask him what his grades were when he was in sixth grade. While grades are important, by the time he gets to high school, they are only part of a wider picture. Community service, extracurricular activities, and teacher recommendations all play into the college application process. It's a shame that grades and test scores have been elevated to such an exaggerated status in so many of our classrooms.

Make certain that you show your approval when your child works hard or comes up with creative solutions to academic problems. "You worked very hard on that poster!" is a much better comment than "Wow! You got a B. That's really good *for you!*"

Nevertheless, it is frustrating for a child who works very hard to rarely, if ever, come up with an A, and the emotions that your child will experience are very real. Help him by pointing out his assets: Maybe Jill aces every test, but Kevin has given hours of his own time to the local senior citizens' group. Emphasize that you hope he will become a good citizen and community member rather than simply an A student. Yes, for some kids, A's will be the ticket to success. Just remind your child that there are many other kinds of tickets.

Some kids are inherently more competitive than others, and if your child's nature leans this way, you can help him find an outlet to compete and excel. Many dyslexic kids find that sports provide an avenue for achievement. In high school, I was a valuable member of our school's track team. Competition is a part of human nature; you can help your child focus his competitive urges in an area other than academics.

## Mistakes Shouldn't Ruin Your Day

*Eight-year-old Sean has told his new friend, Ernest, that he will call him after school so that he can arrange a date to come over to play. The problem is Sean has written down Ernest's phone number wrong, and the number isn't listed in the phone book. Sean is in tears when his mother comes into his room. Realizing that Sean must have reversed the numbers, Susan reassures her son and promises that she will approach Ernest's mom at drop-off in the morning, get the correct number, and arrange for another play date. Sean feels a little better, though he is still angry at himself for messing up the numbers. "How come I'm so stupid?" he asks his mom.*

Kids can be very hard on themselves, so it's your job to make certain that your child understands that mistakes are part of being human. It's important to teach your child early on that many mistakes can be corrected and that he should pay attention to his instincts when he thinks he might be making a mistake.

A simple mistake can send a dyslexic child plummeting into feelings of self-deprecation. He can be feeling great about himself one moment and miserable the next. Parents can help by reassuring their child that a mistake is not the end of the world. Help your child problem-solve to find ways to correct the mistake or to ensure that he will do better next time. For instance, Sean's mom might gently suggest that the next time Sean asks a friend for a phone number he could have the friend write down the number, or he could read the number back out loud to his friend to make sure he has it right. Above all, let your child know that you are not upset or disappointed by his mistake and that you will support him and help him find ways to do better in the future.

## Preparation Is Key

*Twelve-year-old Justin was thrilled as he arrived at summer camp, but he has just found out that he'll be expected to take part in weekly skits. He panics when his counselor starts handing out slips of paper, informing the kids that they'll have 15 minutes to put their impromptu drama together before performing before the larger group. Though the activity is supposed to be fun, Justin is terrified that he'll make a fool of himself; everyone will find out how difficult it is for him to read. He stares in disbelief at the short speech he's supposed to make, but he can't figure out some of the words. With some quick thinking, he approaches his counselor and feigns an upset stomach.*

All parents of dyslexic kids need to be especially vigilant about surprises. Though it may take some extra work on your part, it pays to make sure your child is prepared for situations that may require reading aloud, following directions, test-taking, and doing projects or assignments. He will need extra time to prepare and follow through in a successful manner. Naturally, you won't be able to prepare your child for every surprise that comes along, but in many cases, you can make sure that the teachers, counselors, coaches, and other adults who work with him are aware that he needs some extra attention in these areas. Had Justin's parents thought ahead, they might have asked the camp director what kinds of activities required reading and specifically if any required reading aloud. Arrangements then could have been made to ensure that Justin would have the time he needed to prepare.

Taking the surprise out of surprises not only increases the odds for success but also helps your child keep a positive outlook. When surprises lead to failure, the dyslexic child may feel bad about himself. Limiting the number of surprises in your child's life will help him maintain a healthier emotional balance. Of course, no one can always be in control of every situation, and you must let your dyslexic child know that. We'll talk in chapter 17 about how to prepare for the unexpected.

## You Belong

*Nine-year-old Jared is working in the family den on a science project with two other kids. Eric is great at writing, so he's putting the lettering on the poster. Bettina is a talented artist, and she's drawing a beautiful whale that she intends to paint blue and sprinkle with silver glitter. Jared is sitting in the corner, pretending to look stuff up in books. He's neither a great artist nor a very good writer and so has removed himself from the work. His mom comes in and sizes up the situation. "Jared," she says, "why don't you go online and print out some underwater pictures? I'll help you find a good Web site. Then Bettina can paste them around the borders of the poster." "That's a great idea!" Bettina says. "Can you find some pictures of an octopus and some sharks?"*

Whenever you can, remind your child that the world moves along because of Us and Them. In all parts of life, there are people who have certain skills in one area and those who have skills in another. Though Jared isn't a good writer, he's great at surfing the Web and using computer technology to reproduce images. His mom is right on top of the situation, realizing that Jared just needs some guidance to spur confidence in what he's good at.

Many dyslexic kids have creative or athletic skills that can be tapped. It's important to let your child know that although he has trouble spelling words, he can come up with a creative idea. In this way, the world of Us and Them works not separately but together. I like to use the example of writing this book. While I have ideas and experiences to share about dyslexic kids, I couldn't possibly arrange them in an organized manner or express them clearly without the help of my writer and my editor. But just as I depend on them to help me get my ideas across, they depend upon me for my professional expertise and knowledge. Together, we make it work. In the same way, your child can find individuals who will recognize his talents and who will want to work or exchange ideas with him.

# as your child grows

The gap between Us and Them will never entirely close, but your child can find ways to bridge it. Help him remember that it all starts with being honest with others about his disability. Others can assist only if they know he has a problem; encourage him to be truthful to himself and others about his disability. Sure, there will always be people who won't be kind, but as your child grows, he will increasingly encounter others who will be supportive and in turn will need his support. That's just the way of the world.

Learning to be honest with others and learning to offer and receive caring and support are important life lessons, whether one is dyslexic or not. This give and take is what makes friendships, partnerships, marriages, and other relationships work. While the dyslexic can identify the areas in which she needs help, some people aren't so lucky. It's not always so easy to put a finger on a character flaw or an emotional difficulty, and these things may not be as readily managed as concrete disabilities in spelling and reading.

As your child grows with your support and encouragement, she will begin to understand that even though she may not learn in the same way as everyone else, she is not so different from others after all.

# 7. Not the Same but Not Different

As you experienced when you did the exercises in chapter 5, a person with dyslexia has a unique perspective on the world—as well as unique challenges. In the previous chapter, we explored the concept of Us and Them and discussed some strategies for helping your child bridge the gap between these two worlds. Now I'd like to delve deeper into the underlying emotions your dyslexic child may be feeling as a result of his unique relationship with the world. When you understand these emotions—and why your child is feeling them—you'll be better able to help your child discover the vital role he plays not only in your family but also in the world.

## finding your child's fit

True enough, your child is not the same as all the other children, but he is not so very different either. This is what you must help him understand. You must help your child find his "fit"—in other words, a place where he can be comfortable revealing and acknowledging his dyslexia while at the same time knowing he possesses the capabilities and gifts necessary to succeed among others. Here are five core concepts you can teach him.

## "We Believe in You"

*In a class of 500, Peter is graduating 396. His grades have never been anything to brag about, but today he feels proud of his accomplishments and confident that he will go on to do well in college. He looks out into the audience and sees his mom, his dad, his grandparents, and his two younger sisters; they are all beaming with pride. Peter smiles back and prepares to step forward and receive his high-school diploma. Though he's not among the top of his class, he feels as though he is on top of the world.*

What has made the difference for Peter? Along with caring teachers and a sound education, Peter has the support of his family. Throughout his grade school and high school years, his parents never doubted that their son would succeed. They worked very hard to help Peter, and their efforts have paid off. He's been accepted at a respectable college and has the inner resolve needed to succeed.

When I was a student, I often felt that I was almost at the bottom of the barrel. Like Peter, I was not very high up in class rank at the time of graduation, because my grades were mostly C's and B's. However, both my parents had always believed in me, and that was crucial to my confidence level. Believing in your dyslexic child is an essential key; you have no idea how many doors can be opened simply because of the faith you have in your child.

My dad believed that I would be a professional baseball player, while my mom seemed to realize that that wasn't my personal goal. She was convinced that I could learn, and so she worked tirelessly with me on homework and school projects. Even though I never became a professional ball player, the fact that my dad believed that I could do it made me feel that he cared. He wanted me to reach high, and I'm grateful he helped me do that.

There is no strategy more important than this: *Believe in your child and openly display that belief.* Whether it's a parent, grandparent, teacher, counselor, principal, or friend, each and every dyslexic child needs someone to believe that she can do it and someone to take the extra time needed to make it happen. The doubts that the dyslexic child experiences on a daily basis can be mitigated by the support of a parent or other mentor. Don't make the mistake of underestimating your importance or of thinking that there's nothing you can do. A hand on a child's shoulder and a comment like "You can do it!" or the simple words "I love you" can make a vital difference in whether a dyslexic child (or any child) develops the inner confidence necessary to keep on trying. Tell your child that you know she can achieve her goals: "If we work together, we can overcome these obstacles. Remember when you didn't think you'd be able to ride your bike? Well, you learned, and you'll learn how to do this, too!"

## "Let Go of Your Anger"

*Ten-year-old Timothy experiences severe dyslexia. Each day, he returns home from school knowing that he hasn't been able to do what the other kids can. Reading, writing, spelling, and following directions are all a strain for him. His mom, Cornelia, helps Timmy as much as she can, but she can't be there to support him every moment. When she began to notice that Timmy seemed angry and frustrated much of the time, she located a dynamic kickboxing class that meets twice a week after school. Now, instead of coming home and picking a fight with his little sister, Timmy vents his frustrations in sports class, where he is building his kickboxing skills as well as his self-esteem.*

Your dyslexic child is bound to feel angry sometimes; there's no way to avoid these feelings entirely, but there are ways to redirect them. When feelings of inadequacy mount, it's natural to feel angry, and kids will often lash out at others when this happens.

While I don't have a magic cure that will make anger go away, I do suggest a two-pronged strategy to lessen its impact. The first step is to remind your child of what he does well. We've talked about this before, but it's a method that can be used to address many of the dyslexic child's insecurities. The more you can emphasize your child's positive attributes and talents, the more he will focus on his strengths rather than on his weaknesses.

The second step is finding a proper venue for the anger to be expressed. In Timmy's case, kickboxing did the trick. For other kids, baseball, soccer, cross-country running, skateboarding, or another sport can be the answer. The key is finding an activity at which he can excel, and that may take some research as well as trial and error.

Remember that this sport or activity is something your child should feel passionate about—not something you choose for him or would like him to do. Maybe you'd like your child to be a fencer or a gymnast; but if that's not your child's dream, you have more work to do. Most kids are willing to give their parents a message about what they like to do most. It's our job to listen and follow through without imposing our own goals and aspirations. Your dyslexic child has his own dreams, and by helping him find the path to them, you will also be helping him overcome some of the anger and frustration that he feels because of his disability.

Be sure to talk about anger. "Do you want to talk about your frustration?" you can ask. "I know it seems difficult. Are you angry because you have to work harder than the other kids?" Or "Are you angry because you want to be outside playing instead of doing this worksheet?" Locate the root of the anger and see if you can help.

Maybe a short break from the task at hand will help your child re-focus with more success later.

## "Take Pride in What You Do Well"

*Erica is a dyslexic 10-year-old who has had a difficult year, both socially and academically. The girls in her class have divided up into cliques, and she doesn't really fit in. Although her grades are average, she has to spend a great deal of time on homework. Nevertheless, her parents have allowed her to stay in the all-state choir and to take voice lessons, which is her one respite. Erica is an excellent singer and participates in her school choir and a barbershop quartet in addition to all-state. While she struggles daily in school, she's above and beyond everyone else when she begins to sing; here, she feels her own strength and knows she has her own special talents to offer.*

The dyslexic child needs to find a place in which she can excel. This will give her the core knowledge that although she can't read or write as fluently as others, she does have her own particular talents. Being able to say to herself, "Well, okay, I'm having difficulty understanding the passage they're talking about right now, but there are things I can do well, too," will help her build an inner strength. In Erica's case, singing is the outlet in which she can really shine. Fortunately, her parents realize that even though it takes a great deal of time and dedication, it's worth the hard work to keep Erica involved in what she does best. Were they to limit her involvement in singing because her schoolwork is suffering, the tactic might backfire because voice is the one area in which Erica feels her own strength and self-worth. Without that solid base in which she experiences continued success, facing the daily disappointments and failures of the classroom might become unbearable, and Erica might simply give up on school.

The area in which your child can excel can be sports, the arts, communication skills, or computer use—any arena that gives her a chance to succeed is important. For instance, although I am not exactly at the top of my game when we prepare the school budget each year (I serve on our local school board), I am the member who seems best able to communicate with the public and keep the board on an even keel. When there is controversy or contention, the members look to me to bring matters to an acceptable resolution. I'm the one they turn to when people need to remain calm and focused. Believe it or not, I'm also a great organizer. Each year, I organize a stay-at-home dads' convention outside Chicago. I was among the original founders of this yearly event, and each year, I devote a good deal of time to orchestrating the conference.

## "Learn to Laugh"

*Jill, a 16-year-old dyslexic, struggles daily, but she has a healthy sense of humor and a good support group. Her three best girlfriends know all about Jill's learning disability and try to be there for her whenever they can. Jill has a huge crush on one of the football players, but she always messes up his name. In private, the four girls call the boy Gary Walnut, a name Jill can recall easily. His real name is Gary Walensky, but there's no way Jill can remember it. "Walnut's coming!" her friends will warn as they walk down the school hall, and Jill will burst into laughter.*

Younger children will have difficulty seeing the humor in their situation, but as they grow older, they will begin to realize that it helps to laugh at mistakes and move on. Jill and her friends are a good example. They aren't laughing at the football player's expense (he isn't even aware that they're laughing), but they have a healthy camaraderie that helps Jill deal with her dyslexia, when possible, in a lighter manner.

I suggest that parents approach dyslexia in this way early on. Try not to take everything so seriously all the time—that would communicate to your child that dyslexia is something to be worried about. Since it can't be changed, worrying is really useless. Instead, assure your child that you will help him work on strategies, but that sometimes, it's okay to just sit back and have a good laugh.

One of the steps to getting over the fear of dyslexia is understanding that you can laugh about your mistakes, talk about them, and figure out ways to avoid the same mistakes in the future. Younger kids may be ashamed, but when you see a misspelled word, for example, you can point to the word, smile, and say, "Oh, there's that troublesome word again! Remember? You spelled it wrong last time, too! Let's see if we can come up with a trick to help you spell it right next time."

If the parent is comfortable, has an easygoing manner, and is even able, on occasion, to laugh about a mistake, a child gets the message that this is not the end of the world. This is reassuring to the dyslexic child, who now feels that maybe the problem isn't so bad after all—and that maybe there is a solution. In so many things, humor is key. Most educators recognize humor as a helpful tool, and as a parent, you can also take advantage of humor's healing and helping effects.

## "You Are Not Alone"

*Ted, Rachael, and Joe are three dyslexic students who meet every other week after school at each other's houses to talk over their problems. Once a month, their parents join them for an evening meeting, and the three families have all grown close. Rachael is a bright student who works very diligently; Ted is more of a social butterfly who doesn't excel academically. Joe is an average to below-average student but a talented athlete. They are all in tenth grade and are old enough to talk over their problems openly.*

*Ted is always relieved to hear that Rachael makes mistakes even though she gets good grades. He knows that she's very smart but somehow feels reassured to know that even kids brighter than him have problems. Joe and Rachael enjoy discussing what they call their "blunders" with each other and with Ted and talking about ways they have learned to cope. Recently, Joe located a great Web site where the kids can chat online with other dyslexic students.*

Part of your job as a parent is to help your child reach out to people outside your family, rather than relying on you at all times. This is called building a support network. Peers are a very important part of this network. As your child grows older, it will be easier for him to seek out others on his own. But you can start by helping him, as early as age 10, form a chat group online or making arrangements for informal get-togethers with other dyslexic children. You might try getting in touch with your school's social worker or special education coordinator to inquire about getting a group together—either for children or for the parents of dyslexic children.

It's reassuring for your child to talk to kids who have similar problems. Getting together with others who feel as you do can be comforting. I often chat with several of my dyslexic students about the difficulties we all face; we find that sharing our experiences and trading stories is a validating experience. We laugh together and remind each other that we're not in this alone. We have not only the support of our families and friends who are non-dyslexic but also the support of people who share our disability.

# deepening the bond

The strategies outlined in this book will help you deepen your bond with your dyslexic child. The job of being a parent is not easy—whether your child is dyslexic or not. But especially for someone with a dyslexic child, parenting may seem to require an inordinate amount of time and effort. Take comfort in the fact that the hours you spend helping and guiding your child, offering ideas, and working out strategies will not be wasted. When she is young, she may not realize how important this time together really is, but as she grows older, she will appreciate the time, effort, and belief you have invested in her, and you will reap the reward of a strong, enduring bond with your child.

Of course, guiding and supporting your child does not mean doing the work for her but rather giving her as many strategies and tools as possible so that someday she can accomplish these tasks independently. This is a fine line; you need to offer help without encouraging dependency.

By taking the time to understand how your dyslexic child thinks, to experience the world as she does, and to give her the emotional support so crucial not only to today's achievements but to tomorrow's, you will let your child know that you are committed to helping her succeed. The message you give your child as you help with homework, talk to teachers, discuss her feelings, and find ways for her to develop coping strategies is that you care and that you will be there. As you work together, your bond will continue to deepen, and your dyslexic child will be increasingly equipped to deal with the challenges she will face each and every day.

my perfect child

has dyslexia

# part 3

# 8. The Diagnosis

Diagnosing dyslexia is not a simple matter. The process will most likely involve a number of professionals and a battery of tests. Keep in mind, however, that a conclusive diagnosis is well worth the effort. Once you've identified your child's specific problem areas, you and others will be all the more prepared to help him.

Often, it is the parent who first sees the signs of dyslexia. Although you may suspect that your child has a problem, be sure to enlist the guidance of experts for a proper diagnosis. True, there are Web sites that offer online assessments for parents, but I do not recommend this approach. Diagnosis involves many different areas and levels of expertise. No diagnosis is of use without a clear-cut action plan based on the input of professionals in the field of special services.

In this chapter, I will discuss the different "pieces" that make up an accurate diagnosis for your child. But first, it may be helpful to give you a brief overview of dyslexia.

# a short history of dyslexia

In 1884, Reinhold Berlin introduced the concept of dyslexia, defining it as a condition that occurred when a person of normal intelligence had difficulty reading. At that time, dyslexia was linked to the left hemisphere of the brain, but researchers were focused on the possibility that it was primarily a vision-based problem. In 1925, Samuel Orton, an American neurologist studying soldiers, found that dyslexia resulted when the soldiers suffered left-brain injuries. Then, professional focus shifted to the neurological cause of dyslexia. As

## ADHD and Dyslexia

It's common for parents to be confused by the many terms describing various conditions and learning disabilities. Dyslexia is a subcategory of learning disabilities (LD), and everyone who is learning disabled is not dyslexic. ADHD (Attention Deficit Hyperactivity Disorder) and dyslexia are two separate conditions, although some children may have both. The most common features of ADHD are distractibility, impulsivity, and hyperactivity. The ADHD child exhibits poor attention to tasks, impaired impulse control, and excessive activity and physical restlessness. ADHD is caused by biological factors that influence neurotransmitter activity in certain areas of the brain; like dyslexia, there is frequently a genetic connection. ADHD can be managed successfully with a combination of behavioral therapy, cognitive therapy (also known as talk therapy), and medication (usually Ritalin).

Children with ADHD may be diagnosed earlier than kids with dyslexia because they may be inordinately disruptive in the classroom setting. If a child has both ADHD and dyslexia, most likely ADHD will be identified first. Then, during a full evaluation, dyslexia will also be identified. Both disabilities will then be addressed in the child's Individualized Education Program (IEP).

scientific technology has advanced, researchers have been able to employ PET scans, MRI, and CT scans to investigate how the left-brain area processes information, linking problems with reading, handwriting, spelling, and arithmetic to incomplete neuro pathways in the processing regions located in the left hemisphere of the brain. These regions of the brain were first identified in the 1880s by Pierre Broca (Broca's area) and Carl Wernicke (Wernicke's area).

Over the years, psychologists and educators have become more involved in the study of dyslexia and offer the very necessary social and educational perspectives that had been missing in the past. Today, we still need to include medical expertise to rule out vision or hearing problems and in some cases to diagnose and treat neurological problems. The focus now, however, is primarily on the social and educational aspects of the disability, as we now know that dyslexia is an ongoing condition that can best be managed with strategies that foster success in the social and school arenas.

# three kinds of dyslexia

There are three common kinds of dyslexia: visual, auditory, and a combination of the two. It's important to understand that visual dyslexia does not mean that your child has a problem with his vision, but instead, problems arise when visual images are processed and interpreted by the brain. With auditory dyslexia, the child's hearing is fine, but the brain, once again, has trouble processing and interpreting the information that is heard. I have a combination of the two; some of my problems are auditory, some visual.

In my case, I had always prided myself on my 20/20 vision and excellent hearing, so it was a shock to learn that my brain doesn't always process visual and auditory information accurately. This realization was difficult for me to accept and in some ways quite frightening. Imagine the uncertainty your child may feel when he realizes he doesn't see or hear the way other people do.

# detecting the signs of dyslexia

*Amelia is a bright 8-year-old, but her mother, Delilah, worries about her. She has noticed that when Amelia reads, she tries to block the words with a bookmark and seems to lose her place often. Unlike her two sisters, Amelia doesn't seem to enjoy reading, and she fidgets and squirms when Delilah asks her to read a passage aloud. Amelia reads hesitantly, often mistaking words and seeming distracted, as if she doesn't understand the story line. Delilah isn't surprised when she gets a call from Amelia's teacher, suggesting that there may be a problem. In fact, she was about to call the teacher herself and request a conference. She has noticed lately that Amelia seems to be losing the exuberance she once showed toward going to school each day.*

Frequently, it's a teacher who first notices the signs of dyslexia. Often, the first suspicions arise when a bright child demonstrates problems with reading. This may be a surprise for the parents, who expect their child to do well in school because she has always been, like Amelia, an exuberant learner.

As a parent, you know your child best, and you may be the one to see the first telling signs of low self-esteem (watch for self-deprecating remarks like "I'm so stupid") or to pick up on a reluctance to go to school on certain days. Overseeing homework, you may notice that your child has difficulty with spelling, following instructions, or remembering mathematical formulas. Perhaps she confuses her left and right more frequently than her siblings did at her age. Or perhaps you are on the alert because other family members have been diagnosed with dyslexia, and your child exhibits similar symptoms.

## Signs of Dyslexia

These are some common problems that you may notice in dyslexic children.

- Problems recognizing or spelling words
- Difficulty structuring written work, such as essays
- Problems with spelling
- Reversal of letters
- Poor short-term memory
- Difficulty with proofreading or identifying errors
- Poor auditory comprehension
- Problems with organizational skills
- Poor handwriting
- Short attention span when listening
- Poor word retrieval
- Problems with visual discrimination
- Problems with spatial perception
- Difficulty remembering names
- Slow completion of schoolwork
- Poor concept of time
- Difficulty distinguishing between certain vowel and consonant sounds
- Confusion with symbols and the alphabet
- Problems remembering daily routine
- Poor reading comprehension

(See "Signs of Dyslexia" for other symptoms to look for in your child.)

Testing for dyslexia most commonly occurs in third grade, although sometimes the problem isn't detected until later. If you suspect that your child is dyslexic and he is in the third or fourth grade, request that his school perform an evaluation. The sooner you can get the appropriate professionals working for your child's benefit, the better. It's better for you to seek help and find that your child doesn't really need it than for you to discover much later that your child needed the help but missed out because the adults weren't "on the case." Trust your instincts: In my experience, parents usually know when something isn't right with their child.

## the team approach to diagnosis

Evaluations and diagnosis should be conducted by a team—not just by one individual. Why? Dyslexia is a complex condition, and experts from a variety of fields—including medical, neurological, educational, psychological, and social—are required to make a proper assessment. School systems invariably use a team approach, including input from teachers and other school personnel and counselors. Private evaluations should also provide a team effort.

Why would you want to use a private diagnostician? Most likely, it's because you want a second opinion. Keep in mind that private sources may cost $1,500 to $2,000, if not more. It's your right to have your child tested by the public school system—and federal law ensures that once you begin the process, it must be completed within 90 days. Some parents fear that once they initiate the process, it will be out of their hands if a problem is detected. Remember that you can still talk and work out problems—you, ultimately, are in charge of your child's best interests.

If you're not happy with the school's assessment or if you'd simply feel more comfortable having a second source of information, private evaluations are fine to pursue. But be sure to inquire about the evaluator's experience testing dyslexic children. Just as you'd be certain your surgeon had a history of success, you need to make sure that those individuals assessing your child are very knowledgeable about dyslexia and test for it frequently.

In addition, inquire about the tests used and make sure they are current. You might want to ask your school for a list of suggested tests as a guide for determining whether the private evaluator is using appropriate tools. There are a number of tests the school district may opt to use; the most common are general tests for reading comprehension, visual processing, auditory processing, intelligence, and so forth. It is also very important that the test be conducted in your child's native language; guard against discrimination of any kind.

## the tests used

Testing requires several hours and may even take days to complete. As mentioned earlier, the first round of tests should be conducted by your medical practitioner to rule out medical problems. Hearing and vision tests should definitely be part of this screening.

Examiners will employ a standard IQ test, which measures verbal and nonverbal abilities. The purpose of this is to determine your child's academic potential in order to figure out if he is performing above or below his capabilities and to compare him with his peers. An average or high IQ coupled with poor academic achievement is a clue that something may be amiss. Of course, IQ tests are shrouded in controversy, as is the ability of such a test to determine academic potential. Keep in mind that the IQ test is only one piece of the diagnostic puzzle.

Your child will also be tested in a variety of skills, such as reading, handwriting, spelling, continuous story writing, numbers, and others. Diagnostic skills that will also be assessed include auditory and visual perception, phonological skills (the ability to identify and manipulate individual language sounds), memory, lateral acuity (crossing over from left to right), spoken language, and speed of processing (how long it takes your child to absorb and process information).

Finally, you will be asked to give a case history for your child. This will involve sitting down with the school social worker or other special services personnel to go over your child's medical history, home background, and any pertinent facts or observations that will help to identify his problem.

# preparing for the test

*Bobby is a second grader who has had a number of difficulties this year. His reading skills are way behind, and his handwriting is sloppy and illegible. His teacher, Mrs. Gittleman, is concerned and has contacted Bobby's parents, who are divorced but amicable, to discuss the problems. When she suggests that he undergo testing for a learning disability, Bobby's mom, Carol, is relieved. His father, Arthur, however, claims there's "nothing wrong" and can't see the sense of pursuing special education services. Nevertheless, Arthur agrees to follow the teacher's advice and even concedes that it would be a good idea for Carol and him to sit down with Bobby and talk about what will occur. Above all, they want to make sure that Bobby is comfortable with the testing and that he isn't fearful of what may happen next.*

If the testing process sounds complicated to you, think of what it must seem like to your child. The best way to lessen his trepidation is to talk about it. Sit down with your child and explain exactly what will happen. Let him know that the reason he is being tested is because you and his teachers want him to learn strategies that will help him do better and feel more comfortable in school. Assure him that

## Special Issues for Younger Children with Dyslexia

The most important issue for parents of younger children with dyslexia to address is early intervention so that your child's self-esteem is not eroded by failure in school. Although most schools test for dyslexia at around second or third grade, some experts recommend testing for dyslexia even earlier. I agree that early detection is crucial, but I also fear that testing *too* early may result in some children being improperly diagnosed. These kids may be reversing letters or not reading fluently at this point in their lives for developmental reasons unrelated to dyslexia and may very well catch up later.

Another common issue is that your younger dyslexic child may feel afraid or worried about starting school, or he may feel angry or frustrated until he is able to more fully comprehend what his disability means. As soon as his dyslexia is diagnosed, you can begin the important process of helping your younger child understand that he learns differently. Your main job at this point is to offer love and encouragement and to work closely with the school to ensure that your child's needs are met and that the groundwork for developing a strong support system is laid.

the testing will help him so that he won't feel so frustrated or angry about learning. Let him know that the tests are being conducted so that you and his teachers will better understand how to help him learn.

Emphasize that there is nothing "wrong" with your child, just that he learns differently, so you need to find the best way to help him succeed. Prepare him by explaining that the tests will look at his handwriting, spelling, reading, listening, and other skills. Be sure to stress that there are no "grades" and that he need not be fearful or worried that he will "fail." Explain that these tests are more like "exercises." He should do his best, but he should also understand that there will be no penalty or grade. Some of the tests may even be fun! Assure your child that the examiners will be very nice—remind him that if he needs to get a drink or use the restroom, he should let the examiner know.

Some children will have difficulty sitting for long periods of testing, so be sure to inquire of special education department personnel how they go about administering the tests. Some may have rigid procedures; others may be more flexible, and you may be able to ask that they break the tests into smaller increments. Don't hesitate to ask questions. If you have any concerns, discuss them with the special services department personnel; that's what they are there for.

# a plan of action: the IEP

Once the testing is complete and a diagnosis of dyslexia is confirmed, the special services department will call you in for a conference to discuss the Individualized Education Program (IEP) for your child. (*Note:* The acronym IEP varies slightly from school district to school district. Where you live, the IEP may also be called the Individual Education Plan or the Individualized Educational Program.) No test is useful without this action plan as the result.

The IEP will describe goals and procedures to be followed by your child's teacher. As its name implies, the IEP is an individualized plan for your child. No two IEPs are ever the same, because each learning disabled child has specific needs. As we have seen, dyslexia can affect many different abilities. While the IEP format differs from state to state and from school district to school district, federal law sets certain criteria for IEP format.

This plan will give you a snapshot of where your child is today, goals for achievement in school, a recommendation for related services to help your child, and an overview of how he will be monitored and evaluated. (See "Understanding the Individualized Education Program" on page 104 for more details.)

As the parent, you will be required to sit down with special education personnel each year to reevaluate and discuss your child's IEP to determine if goals are being met and if methods need to be altered. Be sure to be open about your concerns. Some parents opt to bring along an "advocate," especially at the first meeting. This can be a friend who "knows the ropes," or you can hire a professional in the education field, a social worker, or a psychologist who may be more familiar with the terms and be better able to ask pointed questions.

I've attended a number of IEP conferences as an advocate with concerned parents who felt that they needed someone in the field to help them navigate this unfamiliar process and absorb and understand the assessment results. Most importantly, make sure both parents are present. Single parents may want to consider bringing a partner, friend, or advocate. Understanding the IEP is crucial to your child's success. Although your child's teacher will be following the guidelines, you will be able to provide input and help from your perspective as a parent if you are clear on what is contained in this essential document.

# first steps

When you walk out of your IEP conference, take time to think about the diagnosis and process the information. If you have taken an advocate with you, set aside some time immediately after the meeting to discuss what happened and go over any questions you may have. If you've attended the meeting with your spouse, make time to sit down together and compare notes.

Here are the basic points I counsel my clients to look for in their child's IEP.

- A statement of the child's present level of educational performance. This statement tells you where he is right now, before initiation of the strategies set forth in the IEP.

- A statement of annual goals, including short-term instructional objectives. This is the plan for your child for this school year.

- A statement of specific special education and related services to be provided and the extent that the child will be able to participate in the school's regular educational program. In other words, this part tells you what special services your child will be given "outside" of the main program and which parts of the curriculum he will participate in along with his non-dyslexic fellow students. For example, if your son does not need what is referred to as adaptive gym, then his IEP should state that he will participate in regular gym class.

- Projected dates for initiation of services and the duration of services. Do your best to see that the special services your child will receive are stated with as much specificity as possible. Push for stated annual and short-term goals, list of services, initiation date for and duration of tutoring services, and a detailed description of what will occur during those services.

Specific services that your child might require can include the following.

**Speech therapy.** If you see a recommendation like "10 minutes of speech therapy once a week for the year," push for a written description

Before you leave the school, be sure to get the phone number of a person on the special services team whom you can call with further questions. Invariably, I find that parents will have additional concerns in a few days, after they have looked over the material at of what will occur during those therapy sessions. This may include instructions like: work on vowels, verbs, vocal chord work.

**Physical therapy.** Often this relates to fine motor skills. An example may be improving pencil grip to help with handwriting.

**Reading therapy.** This will depend on the child's age. A younger child may focus on learning to read traffic safety signs (by studying a book on traffic safety signs, going outside to look at traffic signs, and so on). Other exercises may focus on improving sight word vocabulary, basic reading and comprehension skills at a pre-stated target grade level (for example, exercises to improve spelling skills to complete sixth-grade spelling tests with an average of 75 percent or higher comprehension; or reading a fifth-grade reading passage silently and answering questions regarding main idea, details, vocabulary, and inference at 80 percent or higher comprehension).

**Math skills.** This is not always included, but you should request that it be addressed with the same level of specificity as in the other areas.

There should be appropriate objective criteria and evaluation procedures as well as a schedule for determining whether the short-term instructional goals are being achieved. Push for having specific dates for checkpoints put into your child's IEP. For example, if services are initiated in September, put in a checkpoint in December. By then, your child may have already achieved a short-term goal, and that portion of the therapy can be concluded or reshaped to target a new goal. Reaching short-term goals helps boost your child's self-esteem and will give both of you an important sense of involvement and accomplishment.

length and absorbed the information. Establishing that communication link before you leave the school will be to your—and your child's—advantage.

In the initial days after the diagnosis, you will be processing what

## After the IEP Meeting

Remember these steps to follow after your IEP meeting.

- Take time to debrief with your spouse or advocate.
- Get the phone number of someone on the special services team who can answer questions you will have in a few days.
- Gather facts and information.
- Talk to your child about his dyslexia (see chapter 12).
- Share information and feelings with your spouse, friends, and family (see chapter 12).
- Keep a positive outlook.
- Meet regularly with your spouse to review progress and share responsibilities.
- Take it slowly and recognize that adjustments take time.

you have learned, sharing information and questions with others, and researching your child's disability. You can visit the online resources listed in the appendix and check your local library for other pertinent books. Keep in mind that gathering information about how to help your child will be an ongoing process, just as his disability is an ongoing element in his life. (See "After the IEP Meeting" for a list of follow-up activities you'll want to do.)

Planning the next steps after a diagnosis of dyslexia is confirmed begins with the IEP, but it is a mistake to think that your own emotional reaction—and your spouse's—doesn't impact the success of the plan. Chapter 9 provides a candid look at taking care of you so you can take care of your child.

# 9. Your Reaction

Even before your child is born, you begin to create the "dream" of what she will be like. You may imagine that one day she'll be a professional tennis player or a famous cellist; perhaps you'd like her to be a gifted scientist or a talented lawyer. Maybe your wish is simply that your child will live a happy, successful life, free from fear or harm. As a parent, you create this dream or expectation and carry it with you. No one ever wishes for a child who will have a learning disability that she will have to cope with for life.

## your emotions

When she's born, your child looks as perfect as any baby. As a toddler, she is active and bright. Your dream remains intact; you have no reason to believe that your child won't be the star you've always envisioned. Most likely, you will have no cause to alter your dream of what your child can achieve until the day that you learn she is dyslexic. What happens then?

With the realization that your child has some kind of learning problem, you see your dreams begin to change. When you receive the actual diagnosis of dyslexia, you may begin to sense that your "dream" child is turning out to be someone you never imagined. You will have to let go of that particular dream and begin again. In a sense, you will have forever lost that image of your child being perfect in every way. As this realization sets in, you may notice a flurry of emotions.

Most likely, this is the first time you've had to squarely face the reality that your child is different from what you imagined her to be. This harsh dose of reality, much like other kinds of loss like a death or divorce in the family, triggers what amounts to a grieving process. The well-known author Elisabeth Kübler-Ross talks about five stages of the grieving process: denial, anger, bargaining, depression, and acceptance. Let's talk about these issues in relation to how you may feel when you learn that your child is dyslexic.

## Denial

*Fred and Anna arrive at their IEP meeting a few minutes late. They have been arguing because Fred didn't think he needed to take the morning off from work to attend the meeting. He is convinced that there is nothing wrong with his son, Jason, who has always been a bright and loving child. The difficulties that Jason has had this year in reading are most certainly the teacher's fault, Fred believes. He is dumbfounded when the learning specialists reveal that Jason is dyslexic. Fred rises in a huff and announces he is going to pursue this with a private evaluator.*

It's not uncommon for parents to respond with disbelief. Even though you have suspected that your child has a learning disability, you may have downplayed its importance or tried to convince yourself that it's simply a developmental delay that will rectify itself in time. When experts sit down with you to tell you your child has dyslexia, your first response may well be denial. "This can't be happening," you think to yourself. "They must be wrong. He seems so smart—how could he be dyslexic?"

There is no harm in getting a second opinion or "shopping around," but eventually you will have to deal with the reality of the situation if dyslexia is confirmed. Some parents may initially tell themselves this is no big deal. They imagine that they'll just work a little more with the child on his homework, and that will be that.

## Anger

*Jeannette can't help feeling angry with her son, Tyler, who has been diagnosed with dyslexia. She had wanted Tyler to go to an Ivy League college and follow in his dad's premed footsteps, but now she isn't so sure that is going to happen. She tries not to reveal her feelings to Tyler, but she often feels so frustrated that his grades are mediocre. There is no way he is going to get into a top-notch college at the rate he is going.*

When denial cannot be maintained anymore, as Kübler-Ross explains it, then anger sets in. It's perfectly normal to feel angry *about* your child, but as a parent, you will need to manage your anger so that your child doesn't feel you are angry *with* him. "Why did this have to happen to me?" you may be thinking. "What did I do to deserve this kind of problem?" You may feel angry with the test examiners or the teachers, or you may be angry at the system for not having better solutions to the problem. You may even be angry with yourself, wondering if there is something you did to cause the problem in the first place. Some parents may feel anger toward their spouse or toward the child. Your anger, particularly if it seems to be directed *at* another family member, must be dealt with or more problems will occur in the family.

As your child grows, your anger may resurface time and time again. Just as your child feels angry that he's not out playing with his friends because it takes him so much longer to study, you may feel angry that you must invest so much time and effort in helping him. At times, it just won't seem fair that this learning disability has eaten up so much of your energies. You may feel just as frustrated as your child with the relentless problems that seem to plague him day after day, with little progress to show for all your hard work.

What can you do to manage your anger? One effective approach is to recognize what is going on and give yourself a time-out. Excuse yourself from the room and go sit quietly in another area until you feel calmer. Stress-relieving activities such as exercise and yoga are also good ways of keeping anger in check.

If you notice that certain situations make you angry time and again, you need to break the pattern. For instance, if sitting with your child each night after dinner and working on homework makes you feel angry about all the time you're spending this way, think of ways to alter the routine. Maybe you need to work with your child earlier, or perhaps you should ask your spouse or a close friend to work with your child a few evenings a week. Perhaps you could try taking a break for cookies and tea at a halfway point or getting up to bend and stretch. The point is that you want to somehow alter the pattern you've been following. If a situation makes you feel repeatedly angered and stressed, it's time to somehow modify your steps.

## Bargaining

*Annette agrees that her daughter, Alexandria, needs extra help at school. She actually feels some relief when Alexandria is diagnosed with dyslexia, because now she understands why it takes her so long to do her homework and why her grades have never been as good as her brother's, even though she is obviously smart. Annette promises herself that if Alexandria can just get through second grade, when the teachers really focus on learning to read, she will be all right. But at her IEP in third grade, Alexandria seems to need even more intervention. Annette is shocked; she had thought the dyslexia would recede as time went on.*

It's easy for parents to trick themselves into believing that dyslexia will "go away." If we work harder with him after school, if we get him extra tutoring, if we practice his math facts with him every night before bed, perhaps this will all work out. Some parents even say to themselves, "If I'm a better parent, this will go away" or "If I stop working so much, this will go away." Regardless of the bargains you fabricate or the "deals" you try to cut, dyslexia is going to remain with your child for life. Yes, there are strategies to help, but the bottom line is that you will not be able to strike a bargain that will alter the conditions that cause dyslexia. You can find books and Web sites that may suggest dyslexia can be cured. I simply don't believe that. Try not to kid yourself; dyslexia is now part of your life.

## Depression

*John can't seem to shake the feelings of despair and sadness he feels each time he sits down to read with his son, Terrell. He was hoping that Terrell would follow in his footsteps and have a love of literature, but it doesn't look like that will happen now that he's been diagnosed with dyslexia. Terrell hates reading; even listening to a story is difficult for him because he loses the thread of the story. John does his best to encourage Terrell and tries to find books about knights or magic that he thinks might interest him. Yet it saddens him to know that Terrell will never really enjoy reading these books on his own.*

Depression or sadness may come and go as you struggle to come to terms with your child's dyslexia. At times, you may feel hopeful and positive, but part of the grieving process involves accepting the sadness you feel about the "dream child" you must relinquish. Like John, you will have times when the fact of your child's dyslexia will evoke a sense of hopelessness and helplessness. If your feelings persist for a lengthy time period (and certainly if they last as long as a year), it's best to seek the help of a family counselor; chances are there are other issues that are troubling you in addition to your child's dyslexia.

## Acceptance

*Lillian has known for several years that David is dyslexic. The mother of two boys, one of whom is a talented pianist, Lillian was surprised to learn that her second child had a learning disability. And at first, she wasn't sure how to handle the news. In time, however, she began to research the disability and found that there are many things she can do to help David. She's not only been an active advocate for him at school but also encouraged David's love of computers. She's signed him up for a number of computer-related camps and courses. She is quite certain that David will grow into a happy, successful adult. Even though Lillian sees him struggling with his schoolwork, her research reassures her that dyslexia is a manageable disability, and she's determined to work with him to achieve his goals.*

Acceptance is the final stage in the grieving process, and although you will undoubtedly backslide at times into denial, anger, or sadness, it's most likely that you will eventually come to accept your child's dyslexia—and even to embrace the knowledge that you will now be able to help. Many parents do feel relief when they learn that dyslexia is the problem, because unlike some more profound disabilities, it is one that can be effectively managed, even though it can't be "cured."

For some, acceptance may take many years, and a small number of parents may never really accept the diagnosis. I know of one dad who, years after the diagnosis, still refuses to believe that his son is dyslexic. He brushes it off and refuses to help the child or pursue information, believing that his child is intellectually "slow" and beyond help. Unfortunately, this child has now begun to turn to drugs and alcohol because of the shame his father's attitude has produced.

It is so important to be aware of your emotional response to your child's diagnosis. How *you* feel about his dyslexia will greatly determine how *he* feels about it. Once you reach the stage of acceptance, you can get down to the business of really working with your child and focusing on his abilities, not his disabilities.

# your emotional response and your child

How will your emotional response affect your child and the relationship you have with him? Let's look at a few possible scenarios.

*Tanya is unwilling to accept that her child is dyslexic. Yes, she's read the papers and attended the IEP conference, but she still isn't buying it. She can tell that Samantha is lazy and doesn't apply herself, and she doesn't think a learning disability is a good excuse. As a result of Tanya's denial, 10-year-old Samantha isn't getting all the help that she needs. Her teachers do as much as they can at school, but without Tanya's support, Samantha is slowed down substantially. Tanya does not know how to "think like her child" and has no intention of learning to do so.*

*Ten-year-old Billy senses that his dad is angry with him. His dad doesn't yell at him or anything, but Billy can't help noticing the way his dad storms around the house when he asks him for help with his homework. His dad tries to help, but within moments, he's frustrated by Billy's confusion and leaves the table cursing. Billy kicks the table and joins his father in an angry outburst. It just isn't fair that this is happening to him.*

*Kay is depressed about Vicky's dyslexia. She's a single, working mom, and she's burnt out by the end of the day. Instead of relaxing when she gets home from work, she has to face Vicky's problems, and it just seems too much to bear. She retreats to her bed with a glass of wine and a book, telling Vicky to call her friends for help with her homework. Nine-year-old Vicky feels guilty and sad because her mother is so unhappy.*

*Ed and Linda take turns working with 8-year-old Eric every night. They have asked his teacher for exercises to use at home to help Eric with his reading, and they brainstorm tactics they can use to help Eric in various situations. Ed and Linda attend a support group for parents of learning-disabled kids and are dedicated to helping Eric do his best. Eric is a bright boy with lots of enthusiasm for learning. He knows that his parents are behind him every step of the way; their positive attitude rubs off on him.*

To maintain a strong, understanding connection to your dyslexic child, you must travel the steps with her. She also is grieving about the child she hoped to be and learning to deal with sadness and denial, anger and frustration, just as you are.

As you travel this path together, think of how important your responses are to her. When you react to her dyslexia with anger, she feels that you are angry with her. When you are depressed and sad, she feels that she should be sad, too. And when you deny her disability, you deny her the help that she so desperately needs from you and from others. She may begin to fear that you are unable to accept her problem and her because her situation is so hopeless.

However, when you respond with acceptance and reassurance, your child's self-esteem grows: She learns that you will support her no matter what and begins to believe in herself because you believe in her. You need not hide your feelings of anger and sadness and frustration (and you can talk to your child about both her feelings and your own). But your actions should be reassuring, supportive, and accepting. As long as your child knows that you love and support her, she will be in a better position to meet any challenge that her learning disability poses.

It is essential to remember that your responses to your child's dyslexia are intricately linked to her own feelings about her disability. If you communicate your confidence and support even while honestly voicing your concerns, your child will surely know that she can master the steps she needs to take. As we pursue the strategies in the following chapters, keep in mind that your child benefits from your active participation both for practical reasons (she'll be able to get things done more efficiently) and for emotional reasons (she'll know you accept her and are there for her). Both are critical to making her secret life a happy life.

# facing the realities

I know it's not easy facing the realities described in this chapter, but don't be discouraged. I know many dyslexic people who are successful, productive members of society, who have learned not just to cope but to thrive. Opportunities, even involving reading and writing, do not immediately disappear because of dyslexia—remember, a dyslexic person wrote this book. This chapter is meant to help you prepare for and understand what you are going through now and will be going through in the future as the parent of a dyslexic child. Much more is possible now that you know what to expect.

I'm also writing as a child advocate. No one will advocate for your child more than you, and if you don't confront your feelings and fears and move on, you won't be there for your child who needs you.

Even as your dreams for your child take new forms, don't lose sight that he also has dreams—dreams for himself but also dreams of you being a good, loving, and supportive parent. Helping him grow and develop helps his dreams, as well as yours, come true.

# 10. Is Dyslexia a Gift?

Some people like to think of dyslexia as a gift: a gift that allows you to see things in a different way and brings out your strengths in certain areas. This, indeed, is true, and we'll talk about the positives of dyslexia in this chapter. I want to be clear on one point, however: I'd certainly like to live my life without dyslexia, and I'm sure your child would, too. But since we can't "send it back," it's better that we take to heart the old axiom "When you're given lemons, make lemonade." Rather than dwelling on the negatives that dyslexia offers, we can look at the positives and try to focus on the ways we can grow as we learn to cope with this disability.

## if this is a gift, i'd send mine back

We all have personal and professional issues we need to work on and improve throughout our lifetime. I don't know of anyone who is perfectly satisfied with every aspect of his or her life. We strive daily to improve our relationships with our spouse or partner, to strengthen our bonds with our kids, to communicate more effectively with our coworkers, or to use our time more productively and efficiently. Developing strategies in order to improve in various areas is a lifelong human pursuit. To accomplish what you want in life, you must take risks and meet challenges.

Dealing with dyslexia is no different. It creates issues that can be confronted and managed. With proper support systems and strategies in place, your child can continue to improve her methods of dealing with her dyslexia throughout her life. Dyslexia is not going to go away, but with your help, your child will be able to find ways to live happily and successfully. Like everything else, it takes hard work, commitment, creativity, and time to develop ways to improve.

After I graduated from college, I had hoped to continue on to grad school and obtain my Ph.D. in educational psychology. Several of my teachers had inspired me, as had my mom, who is an educator herself. Instead, I had taken a job as a bus dispatcher, thinking that my dream to pursue graduate studies was an unrealistic goal.

One bitter cold night, after I had dispatched all the buses and some were returning, I stepped into the parking lot to help direct the bus drivers into their parking spaces. I had chosen this job because it didn't require me to write, and very little reading was necessary. I realized that even though my dream was to go on to grad school, I had purposely sought out an occupation that wouldn't require me to stretch or grow. I can still remember that moment, with the cold winds whipping across my face and the acrid smell of bus exhaust fumes heavy in the air. I had a choice I had to make. I could stand in that bus lot for the rest of my life, wondering why I hadn't pushed myself to pursue my dream, or I could face my learning disability, improve my coping strategies, and resume my drive to achieve what I really wanted from life.

With the damp wind thrashing and another cold night setting in, I knew for sure that directing buses bitter cold night after bitter cold night was something I didn't look forward to doing for the rest of my life. I began to consider if, with hard work and determination, I could go on to get my doctorate. I knew it wouldn't be easy to do. I knew there was no guarantee I'd succeed. I knew I had to find out if I could do it.

Soon after, I asked my mom to help me fill out my application for grad school. I got in all right, then blew my first exam. But rather than just writing me off or waiting to see if I would turn myself around, my professor sent me to the learning-disability specialist, who diagnosed my dyslexia. For an instant, I thought about dropping out right then and there, but I knew I wasn't going to give up that easily.

I firmly resolved that I would get through grad school in spite of my disability. I would work harder and longer than anyone. I would use every strategy I could find to get through successfully, including getting extra help from a learning-disability specialist. Believe me, it was every bit as hard as I knew it would be. I had to work long hours and devote myself entirely to success. But I pulled together all my strategies and resources, stuck with it, and made it. I achieved my dream. Your dyslexic child can achieve his dreams, too.

Dyslexia didn't stop me—and it needn't stop your child from reaching out for success. Every day, I spell words wrong. I reverse letters and numbers. I get directions mixed up or forget a name or date. But each day, too, I spell some words right, get some letters and numbers correct, and end up exactly where I'm supposed to be. The only way to manage dyslexia is to work with it, not against it.

Unfortunately, I can't send this "gift" back. Your child, too, will learn to make lemonade out of lemons, if you help him find the recipe. Here are what I consider the most important ingredients your child will need in order to achieve his goals.

## Persistence

*Julianne is a 10-year-old dyslexic who has decided to pursue swimming. She holds the county record for breaststroke in her age group and hopes to go on to participate in the Junior Olympics. In addition to keeping on top of her schoolwork, Julianne spends hours during the week at swim team practices and often attends meets on weekends. She is a determined youngster who refuses to give up. Though she has to put in extra time to keep her grades up while still swimming, Julianne knows that if she works hard and persists, she will be able to do both.*

I've observed that dyslexics can be extremely persistent people. Often, when I'm on the treadmill and feel like giving in to my fatigue and stopping, I remind myself of how hard I work to achieve other goals in my life—to write a paragraph, to read a journal article, to prepare for a class. Knowing I've succeeded through persistence prompts me to keep on running until I've reached my goal. I know that I've accomplished a great deal simply because of my refusal to give up, and running on a treadmill is no different. Your child may very well develop this same sense of persistence, and you can help remind her of her successes so she realizes how her work has paid off.

## Drive and Ambition

*Trevor is convinced that he will be a politician when he grows up. His first step is running for school office, and he launches an impressive campaign* to be president of his eighth-grade class. Though Trevor is dyslexic, he garners the support of his friends, who help him make posters to line the hallways of the school. He even appoints a PR person—a good friend who is great at putting Trevor's ideas into writing. Trevor also conjures up a scheme to give away free packs of gum along with stickers spouting "Vote for Trevor." He has plenty of solid fund-raising plans to help pay for the eighth-grade dance, as well as ideas to get kids more involved in school spirit. He's well ahead of his competitor and is quite confident that he will win the election.

At times, you may be surprised at how driven your dyslexic child seems, but adversity can inspire strength, and many dyslexic kids and adults view their disability as just one more challenge to be conquered. Once a child decides that he's going to "take on" the problem of dyslexia, he may exhibit amazing resilience. Other kids may never face such adversity until much later in their lives, and they may be unprepared for it. Your child will already know what it means to struggle and overcome obstacles. It's necessary to keep our goals in perspective, of course, and we'll talk more about this issue in chapter 11. But a dyslexic child can accomplish many things if he has a good support system and self-confidence.

## Creativity

A dyslexic 12-year-old, Max is an avid rock collector and has amassed a huge collection. He has joined a rock-collecting club that meets after school and has helped form a rock exchange, where kids can trade their collectibles. Max's mom, Dianne, takes him to every museum and rock or gem exhibit she can find. She's not surprised, one day, to find that he is arranging his rocks on shelves surrounding his room, with appropriate identification tabs under each, a task that will take him hours to com-

*plete. In addition, he has figured out how to use his rock tumbler to make beautiful polished rocks that he turns into stunning necklaces and key chains.*

It's often said that dyslexic kids are extraordinarily creative. I don't know of any scientific studies to support this claim, but I do suspect that dyslexia lends itself to a different way of thinking. It's easy for me to think outside the box, because that's the way my brain normally functions. It's actually difficult for me to put my thoughts back "in the box" to get something down on paper in organized fashion for others to understand. Like Max, many dyslexic kids seek unusual or artistic outlets for their talents, since they often may not excel in the academic world.

## Individuality

*Francine is a 16-year-old with dyslexia who is heading a breast cancer awareness group at her high school. While many of her friends think she's silly to be worried about this issue at her age, Francine wants to raise her peers' awareness by passing out literature and raising money for the cause. Her social studies teacher, Mrs. Woodbine, has encouraged Francine in her quest and even arranges for her to make a speech on the topic prior to the spring concert. Francine convinces a few of her friends to be at the ticket booth to accept donations, which will be sent to support the cause of curing breast cancer.*

What makes some kids unafraid to follow the road less traveled? In Francine's case, her dyslexia has set her apart from others since she was 7 years old, and she is increasingly aware, as she grows older, that there are numerous contributions she can make to society that are not limited by her disability. Francine will never win the school spelling bee, but she very well may become the first student at her school to raise thousands of dollars for the cure of breast cancer.

Even without a formal diagnosis, I understood early on that I was different from other kids. I began to realize that along with my weaknesses, I had my own strengths. I also learned that I didn't need to prove anything to anyone else; the only person I had to answer to was myself. As your dyslexic child gains confidence, he too will realize that he sets his own goals and standards. Yes, he is different—and that is a good thing to cherish and nurture.

# staying positive in a negative world

The very fact that we call dyslexia a "disability" reveals that we do not view this neurological condition as a gift. Nevertheless, like anything in life, we can choose to view dyslexia from an optimistic perspective or a pessimistic perspective (the glass is half full or half empty). Let's take a look at two families' approaches to their children's dyslexia and how their reactions translate to their children's feelings about their learning disability.

## The Glass Is Half Empty

*Serena is devastated when she learns that her son, Toby, has dyslexia. Her sister is also dyslexic, and even though much less was known about the condition when her sister went to school, Serena can't help but feel that Toby will never lead a successful life. After all, her sister ended up in a menial job and barely managed to graduate from high school. Toby senses that his mom has given up hope in him, even though his teacher reassures him that now that his IEP is complete, she has plenty of ways to help him succeed in school. He feels torn between his mom's hopeless attitude and his teacher's insistence that he can do well. He'd like to do well in school, but his mom keeps talking about how Aunt Karla has the same thing and look where she's ended up.*

## The Glass Is Half Full

*When Paul and Gail learn that their daughter, Sharla, is dyslexic, they take a deep breath but don't panic. They already have one dyslexic child and know how much hard work it will be. Dean, their older son, has graduated from high school and is heading for college in the fall. He's majoring in psychology, and they've already arranged for tutoring to help get him through his first semester. Paul and Gail have every confidence that he will succeed, so when Sharla, who is 9, announces that she wants to be a lawyer when she grows up, they take her seriously. After all, she's a bright, outspoken girl, with lots of passion and good ideas. They assure Sharla that they'll do their best to help her, just like they did with her brother.*

I like to remind parents that dyslexia may not be the gift you ordered from the catalog for your child, but you can nevertheless find a way to make sure your glass is half full. Here are a few ways to do so.

- Ask your child about her dreams and find ways to encourage them.
- Respect her individuality.
- Provide outlets for her creativity.
- Find ways to spark and satisfy her curiosity.
- Praise your child's efforts, every day.
- Be proud of her persistence (even if it seems like stubbornness).
- Remember that your dyslexic child, like all children, does have gifts; nurture and honor those strengths.
- Teach her to use her intuition; explain ways that you use your intuition to help you.
- Encourage independence while providing understanding and support.

the program

for success

# part 4

# 11. Establishing Goals

**You've met with the school** to discuss your child's Individualized Education Program (IEP) and worked through your own emotions regarding the challenges that face your child. Now it's time to sit down and figure out how you can work together with your child to help him fulfill his potential and reach for his dreams. Goals are important for everyone; we each need a sense of direction and focus in life so that we can achieve our objectives. Writing down your game plan with your child will help ensure that he stays on target and will also help you keep track of his progress.

## adjusting expectations

When you are faced with the news that your child is dyslexic, one of your first reactions may be to lower your expectations. "He won't grow up to be a best-selling author," you may think to yourself. Or "Well, there goes my dream of my daughter ever becoming a doctor." We have talked about the necessity of facing our dreams and possibly altering our perceptions of what the dyslexic child may become, but lowering your expectations is not the answer. You can still have high expectations and great dreams of success for your dyslexic child.

What you may have to do, however, is adjust your thinking about the manner in which your child is going to achieve his dreams. I admit that I would not make a great neurosurgeon, but my dream of being a college professor might also have seemed crazy to some at first. I didn't lower my expectations for myself. Instead, I decided to keep my expectations high but adjust my plans with respect to how I would achieve my goals. I knew I would have to schedule in more study time than most, that I would have to line up a good support team to help me, and that I would not be able to pull off waiting until the last minute to get my assignments done properly.

Each dyslexic child is going to need help in specific areas in order to reach her potential. The IEP will describe what she needs in order to do her best. Keep in mind that your dyslexic child is getting help in certain areas because she needs it. But also remember that she is capable of success and achievement. With the right tools, your child can set her goals and aspirations as high as she wishes. The key is finding the right strategies and methods to fit her learning style.

# setting goals for success

Working with your child to create concrete goals will give him the road map he needs to find success. Yet the process of determining appropriate goals can be a difficult one. The following strategies will help you and your child to create goals that are workable, specific, and challenging.

## Work with the IEP

Though the IEP is primarily written for teachers to use in the classroom, you can use it at home as a guide for how your child learns best. Working with the school and the diagnostician, you can identify the best learning style for your child and match his goals to that style. For instance, if he learns best by listening, you may want to rent or buy audio books for him to use. If the IEP reveals that he needs extra prep time for reading assignments, you can use that information when helping your child organize his homework schedule. By carefully studying your child's IEP, you will get a good idea of what he needs help with. Help him only with the tasks he can't do—don't offer help in the areas he can master independently. This is important because your child needs to experience success on his own. When establishing goals, make certain that you are pinpointing problem areas that need to be addressed.

## Make Goals Specific

You'll notice that your child's IEP states goals in a manner that is quite specific. This is a crucial key to setting goals your child will be able to achieve. Rather than having him say, "I want to improve in math," help your child phrase his goal in more detail, such as "I want to learn my multiplication tables up to 10 by next Monday" or "I will learn to add fractions by next Tuesday." Write the goal down on paper; post it on the refrigerator or on a bulletin board in your child's room.

What happens when goals aren't specific? Usually, they're ignored and generally just aren't met. The child will wander aimlessly, not sure of how to proceed or where he's going. A goal such as "I want to be a better student" may be overwhelming because it doesn't describe how to begin or where to go. Vague goals aren't helpful for parents or educators, either. It's easy to throw in the towel when you can use the excuse "I didn't understand what they wanted, so I just couldn't do it."

If the goal is not detailed in the IEP, the school, for instance, can say, "Well, he's doing better." Better at what? Goals need to be clearly defined so that they can be assessed accurately. Keep this rule in mind when dealing with the school, as well as when forming goals at home with your child.

## Make Goals Realistic but Optimistic

There is no sense in creating a goal that can never be reached. You want your child to experience progress and success, not to feel bad about herself. This is a tricky step because you also want to be optimistic; you want your child to reach for the stars, but you don't want her to fall flat on her face trying to get there.

Help your child create goals that are realistic and positive. Always write the goal in positive terms: "I will learn the directions to ride my bike to the park," not "I will stop getting lost every time I ride my bike to the park." Positive rather than negative statements will spur your child onward. If you suspect that the goal is too difficult (or too easy) for your child to achieve, gently guide her to a more reasonable outcome. For instance, instead of "I will be the best basketball player on the team this year," help her redefine the goal: "I will make the starting lineup by the end of the season." Instead of "I'm going to graduate high school," perhaps the goal should be "I will graduate in the top 50 percent of my class." Remember, you can always adjust the goal if it's not working.

## Include Your Child

If you are using the IEP as a basis for your child's goals, be sure to include her in the process. She may not understand the wording or content of the IEP, but you can explain to her what the goals are in ways she can grasp. Seek her input on how the goals can be achieved.

For instance, she may say, "If I'm going to read for 1 hour after school, then I will need a 10-minute snack break in the middle." Or "Yes, I do want to get my math worksheets done on time. But I will need to blow off some steam playing outside before I sit down to work."

In order to feel in control and take ownership of the goals, your child needs to be involved in deciding what's important and how to achieve it. Research shows that having choice and control increases motivation and contributes to the successful completion of goals. However, your child's dyslexia may manifest itself in a difficulty with goal-setting and organizational skills. So even though it's important for a child to have involvement and control, the dyslexic child may need more guidance in this area because organization may well be one of her weak areas.

## Consider Both Short-Term and Long-Term Goals

Some goals will be easily met in a short time frame. For instance, learning the alphabet may not take your child more than a few weeks; reading for 15 minutes without a break might take just a few days. Other goals will be ongoing, long-term ones, which may appear on the IEP for a number of years. A goal like "improving listening skills" may be something your child will work on throughout her school years. Along the way, there will be many short-term goals that will be established and met.

## Get Organized

Organization is a key element of goal-setting, for both you and your child. You should keep files on your child's IEP and diagnosis as well as articles, references, and other materials related to his progress (this will also come in handy if he transfers at any point to another school). When you go to the IEP conference each year, take your file folders along. This shows the educators that you are organized, you care about the situation, and you plan to stay on top of it to make sure they are following through. Your file will help you determine if the school is still on target. Although most schools are diligent about following the IEP, there are some that aren't. Chart your child's progress and point it out if the school is falling short in doing its part.

You can also help your dyslexic child with his goals by devising color-coded folders he can use at home in which he can keep materials related to his goals. Another tactic is to make a goal chart, which can be hung on the wall or refrigerator. We'll talk more about this later in the chapter.

## Break the Goal into Small Steps

When you help your child establish a goal, break down the steps that outline how it will be achieved. For instance, if the goal is to "Read my novel for the book report by next Friday," make a list of how that will be accomplished. Draw up a calendar and block in the hours that will be spent reading, including additional time for the weekend as well as breaks or snack times. Figure out how many pages per day your child must read in order to accomplish his goal within the allotted period of time. Younger kids will benefit from posting a chart that graphically depicts progress.

## Set a Time Frame

Drawing up a time frame is also crucial. A goal that hovers in the distant future without any specific end date won't do you or your child much good. When forming the goal, estimate how much time your child will need; remember, you can always adjust the goal later if necessary. Start out with the idea that your child will achieve the goal within a limited time. This gives him the impetus to get started and stick with it.

# assessing and tracking goals

Along the way, assess your child's goals. Is progress being made? Is the goal still realistic? How can it be altered if need be? Be sure to include a plan for measuring your child's success. How will he know when he has reached his objective? For example, will success be measured by scores on a test at school or by self-appraisal?

If your child encounters trouble, encourage him to adjust the goal. Some goals seem possible at the onset, but unforeseen problems can arise. If that's the case, help your child assess the goal and redefine it. For instance, if he set out to create a large-scale model for his science project but finds the materials he has chosen aren't working, you can try creating the project on a smaller scale, using different materials. The goal is still there, but it has been adjusted. Be flexible and offer your child constructive feedback. If the goal isn't achievable, sit down together and determine what you can change to make things work.

## Make a Goal Chart

*Ed, a sixth grader, has a book report due in 6 weeks. He and his mom sit down to work on a goal chart. The objective is to read the book and write the report on time. The "outcome" is to get the assignment done with Ed understanding what he reads and what he writes. They decide they will know he has accomplished the task when an independent tutor (in this case, his dad) reads the report and finds it acceptable.*

*Ed and his mom map out a plan. He will read 30 minutes each day, leaving 2 weeks for the writing of the report. As Ed reads, he will sit at the computer and type in the important points of each chapter, or he will talk into a tape recorder, whichever he finds works better. Each day, he will go over his computer or taped notes with his mom to make sure he has understood what he is reading and is following the main points correctly. Once the book is finished, he will sit down with his mom to make an outline of the book report, following instructions handed out by the teacher. Ed then will write a rough draft of the book report and go over it with his dad. His dad will make some suggestions, and Ed will then rewrite the report. Ed will use spell check on his computer and then his mom will*

## Your Child's Goal Chart

Here's a goal chart for improving handwriting. It incorporates every aspect of good organization for your child: reasonable goals, longer-term goals broken out step-by-step, a time frame for progress, and the means for evaluation.

**Goal/objective.** Form handwriting letters more clearly.

**Reason/outcome.** So people can read what you write. We care because writing is an important mode of communication.

**How we will know we are there.** Pre- and post-measurement assessment. An outside viewer (grandparent, for example) will look at the handwriting and see if it is better than before. Can he read 45 percent or 90 percent of what you write? Be specific and quantitative.

**Plan/time frame.** Spell out the process in detail.

Step 1. Get handwriting book, work on fine motor skills, use templates.

Step 2. Practice ½ hour each day for 6 weeks.

Step 3. Evaluate progress and have someone review progress twice a week.

Step 4. Post-measurement assessment.

*double-check his work. He will also ask the teacher to see if she will pre-read the report and make suggestions. He will then complete the project, his father will give it a final review, and Ed will hand it in on time.*

See "Your Child's Goal Chart" for an example of a goal chart. You can use this as your format or make up your own. Just remember to include the key elements of goal/objective, outcome (what you hope to achieve and how you will assess it), a detailed plan, a time frame, and adjustments. Place the chart in a location or file that's easy to see or find.

## Motivate and Reward

How can you motivate your child to achieve his goals? The fact is, the best motivation comes from within; this is called intrinsic motivation. Extrinsic motivation, such as rewards like toys or candy, can work now and then, but don't depend on them. The noted author Alfie Kohn talks about this issue in depth in his book *Punished by Rewards*. He points out that the best way to motivate your child is to make the project or goal interesting, provide choices, and offer creative ways to spark curiosity. For instance, if your child has a science project and you offer him a marker and a poster board, he's less likely to be enthused than if you say, "Let's get some glitter, marbles, construction paper, and whatever else you can think of and work together to make a cool solar system!" Also, I'd suggest that you give your child plenty of encouragement. Verbal praise goes a long way.

Remember, however, that you can't motivate someone to do something that she just can't do. For instance, no matter how much money you offer me, I will never play basketball for the Chicago Bulls; I'm just not good enough. Likewise, if your dyslexic child cannot read aloud without stumbling, you will not get her to do so by threatening or offering bribes. In fact, this will most likely only make

My son, Kevin, is intrinsically motivated. He'll get interested in a subject if I pose a challenging question. My daughter, A.J., responds best to an extrinsic reward—a trip to the video store together or a special treat. The key to motivating your child is knowing what works for him, whether it's whetting his intellectual appetite or using stickers or other extrinsic motivators.

One way to motivate your dyslexic child is to explain the goal. Sometimes dyslexic kids just don't see the point of what you're trying to teach. Identifying at the outset where the assignment is going and what you hope he will learn from it helps your dyslexic child focus on and become excited about the learning outcome. Sometimes dyslexics just can't see the forest for the trees.

I favor trying to teach kids intrinsic, rather than extrinsic, motivation. Words of encouragement such as "I believe in you!" or "I'm so proud of you that you figured out this problem" or "Mommy and Daddy appreciate what a great help you are to the family when you set the table" are preferable to offering a piece of candy or extra TV privileges. Do try to foster intrinsic motivation in your child, but don't consider it a failure if you also sometimes use extrinsic motivation. In these instances, try to use rewards like stickers or extra time doing a favored activity—lollipops are a last resort!

her reading worse. But a good coach, teacher, or understanding parent can help a dyslexic child to do her best and perform to the best of her ability. This is true of any child.

This is a fine line, because your dyslexic child does need to be challenged, and she can achieve many things. If you are in doubt about what she can and can't do, go back to the IEP and study her weak areas. Yes, there will be problems that will seem nearly insurmountable and will not be conquered in a few days or even a few weeks. Certain weaknesses will be with your child all her life. But there are areas that can be developed and goals that can be reached. Your child may not be able to win the spelling championship, but she may be able to win the prize for most original short story. She may not get the lead role in the school play, but perhaps she'll design the sets that help make the play a huge success. With your help, your dyslexic child will be able to achieve many of her goals—even those that may now seem out of reach.

Now is not the time to abandon goals, but it is the time to realize those goals may require more work and attention than you may have first thought. You can still aim high, just aim well!

# 12. Next Steps: Putting Together Your Game Plan

**Once you learn** that your child is dyslexic, you may be tempted to keep your knowledge a secret, just as your child will often try to keep his secret life to himself. But the first step in your game plan should be exactly the opposite; open your mind and heart and step confidently into your new life as the parent of a dyslexic child. You need to talk to others, seek information, and gather support. (We'll talk about the support system in chapter 13.)

## telling your child

As soon as possible after receiving your child's diagnosis, talk with him one-on-one about what you have learned. This will give you a chance to offer your child explanations for what he has been experiencing—and give him a chance to ask questions.

I have found that the best way to present the problem is to give a short definition of dyslexia but follow it up with personal examples that your child can easily understand. For example, "Remember the time you got mixed up with the directions to your classroom? That is an example of dyslexia. Your brain takes in the information, but sometimes it scrambles it up." The special services team will describe your child's individual problems to you; in turn, you can discuss each issue with your child at home.

Assure your child that he is very intelligent and that you will work with him to find ways he can learn best. You might tell him about this book: "The book I'm reading now is about a college professor who is dyslexic. He had lots of trouble in school for a while, but his parents and teachers helped him, and he grew up to write books and teach others about dyslexia." You can also mention famous actors, writers, or musicians who are dyslexic to let your child know that he can be successful and that other people share the condition. (For a list of famous people with dyslexia, visit the www.playback.net web site listed on page 249 of the Resources section. Your child may find this especially inspiring.)

Answer your child's questions honestly and encourage him to talk about his fears and other feelings. Make sure you approach him as soon as you can; don't wait because you think he's "too young" to understand. He needs to know that he has a unique learning style, that he needn't be ashamed, and that you and others will be there to help him. I recommend explaining the condition to your child over several sessions, because it's a lot of information for him to absorb at once.

Instead of just hearing about dyslexia, some children might benefit from graphic explanations. So give your child specific examples he can relate to. For instance, you could say, "Remember when I

The most important key to communicating well with your child is honesty. Of course, how much detail you provide depends on your child's age; a younger child will need information explained in simple terms, while an older child requires a more detailed explanation. If he does not take in information well aurally, you may need to provide drawings, pictures, or diagrams as visual aids.

On a day-to-day basis, communicating with a dyslexic child may mean that you have to repeat instructions or present instructions visually (using charts or pictures), especially if you are giving multiple or sequential directions. Another tactic is to ask your child to repeat the instructions back to you so you know that he understands. Older children, however, may not like this method, so use it only when you feel it is particularly necessary.

Always keep your child in the loop. If you have a meeting scheduled with a teacher to discuss his homework or a progress checkpoint, let him know about it. Provide him with positive feedback on a daily basis. Children need to hear about what they are successful at as well as what they need to work on.

stopped you as you were reading yesterday and pointed out that you had said 'hospital' instead of 'hotel'? That was because of the dyslexia." Or "The other day when we went to visit Aunt Mary, you wanted to take a right instead of a left in her apartment building, even though we've been there many times. That was because of the dyslexia."

In later years, your child might be invited to attend portions of his annual Individualized Education Program (IEP) meetings. It's particularly helpful to have him present when the team is discussing how the IEP will be implemented. Often, the child will offer valuable input or ask pointed questions.

# explaining to siblings

Siblings may be very concerned about why their brother or sister is having trouble in school, particularly if they are older. Younger siblings may not really grasp the problem and may not understand what dyslexia means until they are older. It's best to explain the diagnosis to siblings in a clear, concise manner. Most kids will be eager to help, but you will need to supervise to make sure they are not doing the homework or other tasks for their dyslexic sibling. Encourage them to help their brother or sister without "doing the work" for them.

When siblings fight (as they invariably do), they may accuse their dyslexic brother or sister of being "dumb." However, if you explain dyslexia clearly, siblings will not really go too far with this, because they will know it's not true. Bring your other children into the loop—let them know what dyslexia entails and give them opportunities to be supportive. Discourage comparisons and competition as you assure each child that everyone has strengths and weaknesses.

# telling your relatives

Some parents may be tempted to keep their child's dyslexia a secret from relatives such as grandparents, aunts and uncles, or cousins. But the best tack is to be open with the family and explain to them what dyslexia is and how they can help. They may be interested to learn of the familial aspect of dyslexia and may even be able to point you to other relatives who have been diagnosed with or exhibit the symptoms of dyslexia. You may want to explain that most of the time, they won't even know that your child is dyslexic, but in certain situations, they may notice he has more difficulty than other children. For instance, you can explain that your child has difficulty following directions, reading aloud, or remembering names. This will help your relatives in their dealings with your child.

Communicating with your spouse or partner about your child's dyslexia and your child's best interests is an ongoing process that requires honesty, openness, and a time commitment on the part of both parents. I suggest sitting down with your spouse on a weekly basis to go over the details of your family life: Remember, little things do count.

Discussing your child's daily concerns (problems with schoolwork, peer and social relationships, and so on) is essential so that both parents know what's going on and possess the information necessary to be actively involved in creating solutions. Dealing with minor problems and learning to talk about them will also prepare you for coping with larger problems, should they arise.

One of the most important aspects of communication is learning to listen. A good way to indicate that you are actively listening is to reflect back what the person you are talking with has just said. Saying something like, "What I'm hearing you say is that you don't feel you can devote more time to helping with homework" gives your spouse a chance to further explain his or her concerns without feeling defensive. Try not to interrupt. Even though you may disagree with your partner, hear him out to the end. You will get your turn to state your views.

Show your respect for your partner at all times; don't let communication become an opportunity for attacking your partner. Avoid broad comments like "You never" or "You always." Use "I" statements instead. For

Be sure to inform your relatives that your child is of average or above-average intelligence and that they do not need to treat him any differently than they would any other child. However, you can ask them to help in areas in which your child has special learning needs. For instance, if Grandma is baby-sitting, she will need to know that she may have to repeat directions slowly or that your child will need extra time when doing her homework. It's instance, you can say, "I feel disappointed that you promised to be at Ramone's game and you didn't show up" rather than "You never come to Ramone's games!"

Pay attention to body language and nonverbal cues. If your spouse is avoiding eye contact, crossing his arms, or rolling his eyes, this may not be a good time to talk. Timing is crucial, so take it seriously. Try not to schedule a discussion when you are hurried or tired. Plan a time when you can both sit down and devote your full attention to the conversation. Say, "Can we talk for 10 or 15 minutes after Ramone goes to bed tonight? I've been thinking about something and would really like your input." Pinpoint in advance the goal you want your discussion to reach and then shoot for it. Set a time limit for these kinds of discussions; then, if you find that you need more time, schedule a follow-up talk for another day.

During the conversation, try not to blame or accuse your spouse. (Also, if you or your spouse get flustered or angry and the conversation goes south, agree to drop it for the time being and make a time to come back to it.) Try to reach a conclusion and devise a specific action plan that includes responsibilities for both partners. For instance, you might decide that mom will work on homework with the child on weeknights, but dad will take over on the weekends, or vice versa.

Remember that children learn communication skills from their parents, so do your best to model an open, honest, nonconfrontational style.

best if family members can be informed and guided; this is in the best interests of your child.

# telling friends

Much of what I've said regarding relatives applies to friends, too—yours as well as your child's. If you explain dyslexia to your child clearly and early on, he will be more comfortable letting other kids know about his problem. My daughter has a friend with a learning disability, and she's very curious about it. She asked why her friend was required to read only two books instead of three during the marking period and wondered if this was fair. When I reminded her of the time it takes me to read a book, she understood that for this child, less work is still a lot of work. She decided to talk to her class-mate about her disability and find out if she could be of help.

Often friends are curious about dyslexia. Kids may be afraid to tell their peers because they think they may be ridiculed, but usually once friends understand what dyslexia is, they will choose to be com-passionate rather than critical. Being honest is the best policy. Giving your child the words to use when explaining dyslexia to her friends will clear up misunderstandings and enable others to offer support.

# working with your spouse

Communication is the key to many problems, and it's crucial that couples keep the lines open when their child is diagnosed with dyslexia. My first book, *Parenting Partners*, devotes an entire chapter to the topic of communicating with your spouse.

For the parents of a dyslexic child, it's critical to be "on the same page" when it comes to communicating about your child's disability. If one parent denies the seriousness of the problem while the other works overtime to try to come up with solutions, your child will not get the support she needs. For one parent to be shouldering most of the responsibility is an overwhelming task. Using a "tag team" effort is best. By this, I mean that one parent takes over when the other needs relief and vice versa. Perhaps Dad is better at language arts, and Mom is better at math; decide who will be the helper for your child according to your own strengths. Make sure that each parent is involved in school issues, such as the IEP conference, and that you are each fully informed about your child's disability. It's tempting for one parent to say, "Well, my wife takes care of the homework" or "I'm not sure what's up with his disability, but my husband follows that closely." It's best if both parents are involved and aware; that way, one can step in to give the other relief whenever it's needed.

Try to maintain a united front. Kids can sense when parents are not in tune on an issue, and they may respond by dividing you even more or by going to the parent who demands less from them. Set aside time to sit down each week as a couple and discuss the issues that need to be addressed. Talk about how to divide your child-rearing responsibilities equally, so that neither partner feels overwhelmed. This is vital in any family but is especially so in families where a child has a disability. Each parent needs to contribute and feel responsible. If you are a single parent, you will need to establish a strong support system. We'll talk more about this in chapter 13.

# 13. Getting the Support Your Child Needs

It may be difficult for you or your child to adjust to the idea that it's okay to ask for help, but this is a crucial step in learning to live with dyslexia. In our society, we value independence and self-reliance, and it may go against your nature to be in a position in which you must ask for assistance. If you want your child to reach his best potential, you both must shed this resistance to support from others. Garnering a support system is one of the most important steps you can make toward helping your dyslexic child succeed in life.

## build your child's team

I don't deny anyone support-team status; everyone you meet can be of potential help. Of course, your child's core team will consist of his parents, teachers, tutors, coaches, friends, and relatives, but you can find valuable support just about anywhere. A good support person is one who is patient, understanding, and capable of the tasks that your child can't do. For instance, my core support team includes my wife, my colleagues, and the secretaries in my office. These are people who are genuinely interested in helping and who can do what I can't: They can spell, organize, and write well. In putting together this book, for instance, I worked closely with my writer, editor, and editorial advisors. Most dyslexic children will need at least one support member who acts as an editor. Since reading, writing, and spelling are areas of weakness for people with dyslexia, your child will need to find someone who is willing to help in these areas. When I was in grad school, I found other students who were happy to proofread my papers now and then, and I also connected with Sharon Silverman, Ed.D., a learning-disabilities specialist who helped me organize many of my papers and who has helped with this book.

Though your child may depend mainly on you right now, you can help him find others who will be supportive. As he grows older, he will seek these individuals out on his own and develop the instincts to discern who will be good support-team members and who will not.

# work with the school

*Pat is horrified to learn that her son, a third grader, is being teased at lunch hour because he has a learning disability. Her first impulse is to call the principal and the head of the special services department and let them have it. After all, it says right in Dennis's IEP that he needs frequent positive feedback to promote his self-esteem, and allowing him to be placed in a social situation in which he is teased or bullied is certainly not what is needed. Pat calls her husband at his office and asks him what he thinks they should do. Jay, who has a calm, yet firm manner, volunteers to call the school and make an appointment to discuss the problem. He feels it would be better to speak one-on-one with the special services department and teacher than to call up the school ranting and raving.*

Among the key players in your child's support team are his teachers and your school's special services department. Working with the school can be tricky, but even if the school falls short of your expectations, try to avoid entering an adversarial relationship. It's crucial to keep the lines of communication open. While monitoring your child's progress and making certain that the school adheres to the recommendations of the IEP, try to be gently persuasive, patient, and persistent. Most educators will go overboard to help your child, but you are bound to encounter difficulties from time to time. When this happens, keep communicating. Don't give up; the school is an essential part of your child's support team.

In the case mentioned above, Jay's approach is bound to be more productive than Pat's. The idea is to keep the school support team on your side and to work together for the best interests of your child. Accusations and demands are less likely to be fruitful than are reasonable methods of communication and compromise.

Help your child to identify teachers who will be supportive. One teacher will be willing to stand by a child in class and calmly help him as he reads aloud. Another will stand tapping her foot, impatiently prompting, "Come on, come on." One teacher will find a child in a hallway and say with concern, "You look lost." Another will demand, "Where's your hall pass?" Find out who the supportive teachers are and request that your child be placed in their classes. If this isn't possible, encourage your child to seek out these teachers for after-school help or to join after-school clubs in which they may be involved. Being around supportive people is good for your child.

# focus on abilities,
# not disabilities

*Eileen, a dyslexic fifth grader, joins an after-school club that is supervised by the language arts teacher. Mrs. O'Leary is well aware that Eileen is dyslexic and has her doubts about whether she has the ability to work on the school newspaper. Eileen convinces her that she's a good reporter because she is curious and knows how to ask pointed questions. She volunteers to conduct several interviews for the upcoming issue and tells Mrs. O'Leary she even has a tape recorder she can use. Mrs. O'Leary is hesitant. "Are you sure you can do this, Eileen?" she asks. Her inclination is to assign the reporting to one of the kids who always gets A's in English and to give Eileen a less important task, such as working on writing headlines in a group with other students.*

It's impossible to shield your child from all the unpleasant, unsupportive people in the world (and you wouldn't want to), but it's important to seek out positive people who have optimistic outlooks. Beware of individuals who want to focus on your child's disabilities rather than on her abilities. There are people who will always be reminding your child of what she can't do—encourage your child to spend more time with those who accentuate what she *can* do. One of the reasons I went into the education field is because it is filled with positive, supportive people. At the college where I teach, very few people complain, "How can you teach a class without writing on the board?" Instead, my colleagues make positive comments about my skills with my students and my adeptness at teaching in a variety of ways. This is the kind of atmosphere that any person, and perhaps particularly a dyslexic individual, needs in order to do her best.

In Eileen's case, it's unfortunate that the school advisor isn't more supportive, but with some prodding, she will probably give in to

Eileen's request. A less confident child, however, would most likely be unable to present herself in such a positive manner and would indeed end up with a less challenging assignment because of the teacher's attitude. You can teach your child to beware of individuals who underestimate her capabilities and encourage her to gravitate toward people who are encouraging. When she does encounter people who doubt her abilities, help her find ways to explain what she is good at and what she needs help with. Teach her to follow her instincts.

## How to Find a Good Therapist

If you decide that you or your child (or both) could benefit from the help of a therapist, it's important to do some research to make sure you find someone who will really make a difference. An essential factor is whether you and your therapist are a good "fit." If the therapeutic relationship is to work effectively, you must be able to trust your therapist and vice versa. If you're uncomfortable revealing your innermost thoughts or you feel the therapist is being unfair or judgmental, you're not going to get very far.

The first step is to collect some names of possible therapists. In my experience, just about everyone knows a good (or bad) therapist these days, so ask around. If you're uncomfortable asking friends or family members, you can seek suggestions from your physician, pediatrician, or community mental health facility; you might also call a hotline number listed in your local yellow pages under "Mental Health."

Once you've collected several names, give two or three a call and see if you can talk to them on the phone or in person to describe the particular issues you and/or your child hope to address in counseling and to find out something about their approach. Ask the therapist if he has handled cases like yours and how often. What experience does he have in

# enlist the aid of coaches and others

*Gene, a Cub Scout leader, has a group of 10 active boys in his den. They meet after school in his basement and work on their scout requirements. He has noticed that Lamont is easily distracted and seems to have some learning problems. In fact, Lamont is dyslexic. Gene makes sure that Lamont has plenty of tools and art supplies to work with because he has noticed that he works well with his hands. While some of the boys are better*

helping dyslexic children or parents with dyslexic children? If your child is suffering from separation anxiety, for instance, and the therapist has never treated a child with this condition, keep searching. Play therapy and art therapy are also great options for kids—ask the therapist you're interviewing about these approaches.

If you are looking for a counselor for yourself and feel you may need medication as part of your therapy, such as anti-anxiety or anti-depressive medications, be aware that your counselor may refer you to a psychiatrist, who has a medical degree and can write prescriptions.

Make sure the therapist is licensed. Also find out what school the person attended, what focus of study he or she received a degree in, and how long he or she has been practicing. If you're dissatisfied with the answers, keep searching. Remember that making the decision to consult a therapist is an important step; you want to make sure that the person you select is the right person for the job.

Once you've made the commitment to begin therapy, follow through and do the homework, so to speak. Therapy is rather like playing an instrument—you have to practice. So when your therapist makes a suggestion, give it some thought, and then give it a try.

*at writing skits or making posters, Lamont does best when he is putting things together and taking them apart. Gene is tuned in to Lamont's needs and makes a special effort to keep him engaged by giving him projects that he can do well.*

In addition to teachers, your child will encounter other influential adults who will be able to help him in life. Gene is one such individual. Although he is not aware of the precise parameters of Lamont's problem, he has a general understanding of what dyslexia is and is curious to learn more. He has talked to Lamont's parents several times about the boy's particular needs.

Over the years, your child will develop the ability to identify caring, helpful people without your assistance. For now, you should be actively involved in finding individuals who will offer support and positive input. Scout leaders, music teachers, coaches, and others· who work with your child in various capacities can all be potential members of your extended support group. Move toward people who treat your child with respect—the music teacher who says, "Let's try that again" rather than "No, that was wrong!" or the soccer coach who jokes, "I mean your *other* left, Buddy" not "Hey, you're going right when I said left!" When I coached a soccer team, I'd often hold the right hand of a child who did not know his right from his left to show him.

Asking for help has taught me a valuable lesson about thanking others. Every relationship involves both giving and taking, so encourage your child to say thank you to those who help him and to offer help when he can. As your child learns to ask for and receive help from others, he will also learn how to offer help and give support. This is an essential lesson for every child to learn.

# broaden your child's support base

Help your child broaden his support base each day. Neighbors, store-keepers, school secretaries, nurses, tutors, coaches, librarians—any person your child encounters can potentially become a support-team member. These people can give your child directions, spell words for him, look up a phone number, or read a passage he doesn't understand. When I was younger, I used to show the clerk at the grocery store my list and say, "My mom asked me to get 2 percent milk. Is this the right item?"

Just remember, however, that people won't always know what kind of help to offer if they don't know what is needed. This is why honesty and openness about dyslexia are so important. Teach your child, no matter what his age, that it is okay to ask for help (even if it's a store clerk or the person waiting in line behind him) and not to worry that it means revealing his so-called flaws and weaknesses. Everyone has them, and while your child may need help in one area, he also has strengths and will likely become a support-team member for someone else in some other way.

To help your child understand this process, be conscious of ways in which you ask others for help and share these with your child. For example, you might take your child to the service counter at the cellular phone store and let him see you ask for an explanation of how to program numbers on the speed dial. Or you might have him see you post an e-mail question on a Web site or stop at a gas station to ask or confirm directions. Look for ways in your everyday life to show your child that everyone has to ask for help—grown-ups, too.

It is my experience that although there are plenty of people who don't care to or don't know how to help, there are far many more individuals who will open their hearts to your child.

# 14. Boosting Your Child's Self-Esteem

**Self-esteem is a crucial issue** for all children; we want our children to feel good about themselves so they can do their best. For the dyslexic child, self-esteem is an especially sensitive area because many dyslexic kids are treated as if they are not "smart," particularly by those who don't understand the nature of the disability. Acceptance by peers and family can also affect self-esteem. A child who feels the unconditional love of his family and friends is more likely to feel good about himself than one who feels he is loved or accepted only when he lives up to certain standards or behaviors.

Your child's self-esteem will depend, in part, on your approval, so your support is essential. Taking the time to read him a book or give him a hug shows him that he's important to you. In addition, self-esteem comes from pursuing what's important to *him*—what does *he* value, what are *his* interests? In this chapter, I'll look at how you can help build and boost your dyslexic child's self-esteem.

# why is self-esteem important?

Good self-esteem helps a child to be confident and affects an array of elements in his life. With a solid sense of self-esteem, he will feel confident about trying new things, get along with others, and be more likely to do well in school. Self-esteem is at the base of our accomplishments in life; without it, how will your child have the courage and confidence to strive for his goals? Here's how to make sure your child gets his share.

**Catch it early.** Primary intervention is important when it comes to self-esteem. The earlier you can start helping your child build a solid sense of his own value, the better. That is one reason why early diagnosis of dyslexia is so important. The sooner you can identify the problem and help your child find strategies to build his skills and raise his confidence level, the more solid his sense of self-esteem will be. Children who struggle with failure for years before they are diagnosed have a decided drawback; it will be harder to catch up, though it is possible (I'm living proof!).

**Know that words make a difference.** When I was a child, little was known about dyslexia or, for that matter, about the importance of self-esteem. Some of my teachers believed that I did not do well in school because I was "dumb" or "lazy." When I was in sixth grade, my teacher berated me in front of my classmates, calling me "stupid" when I couldn't come up with the answer to her question. I remember sitting in the back of the class, with all the other children turned to look at me, as she accused me of being stupid. This was a traumatic experience that I will never forget. While I can no longer recall the exact question she asked, the feeling of embarrassment and frustration I felt at that moment is indelibly etched in my memory.

Parents tend to blame themselves for their children's problems. When you feel yourself falling into the trap of blaming yourself, try to give your internal messages a positive spin.

- Instead of "I don't think he can do this," say "Let's try a new approach."
- Instead of "I can't keep helping him," say "If I keep trying, he'll eventually get it on his own."
- Instead of "I'm tired of this," try "It's time to take a break."
- Instead of "Other parents don't have to do this," try "Other parents have other issues."
- Instead of "I'm a bad parent; this is all my fault," say "I didn't do anything to cause this problem."
- Instead of "Maybe so-and-so is right. He really is dumb," try "I know that's not what his evaluation says."
- Instead of "Why did this happen to me?" try "This isn't about me."

Today, thankfully, we have come a long way in understanding that what we say to our children is extremely important in developing their sense of self. Words of encouragement and confidence are essential to children. Empty praise isn't the object, though. Instead of saying, "You're the best kid in the whole world," encourage your child in honest and specific ways. "You really studied hard for that math test. You must feel proud that you put so much effort into your work!" Remember to praise the effort, not just the outcome. You can offer kudos when your child completes even a small step toward a goal.

**Recognize the importance of actions.** Children are very intuitive, and dyslexic kids are especially so; your dyslexic child may easily spot when someone is being insincere. Remember that your attitude is very important in shaping your child's self-esteem, and your actions will speak even more loudly than your words. If you tell your child he's great but then ignore him or fail to help him find the skills to deal with his dyslexia, he'll doubt your sincerity, and his self-esteem may plummet.

If you want your child to think that school is important, go to his school and get involved in his education. If you want your child to know that you think he's an excellent soccer player, go to his games and be there when he kicks that winning goal. Show your child that you value him by supporting his activities and interests.

**Adopt an effective parenting style.** Parents who are both democratic and strict help a child live and grow well. They set clear, consistent rules and limits so that the child knows what is expected of him. When a child knows what to expect, he feels more in control. Parents who set rules and limits are letting their child know that they believe he can follow them and that they care enough to provide boundaries. For dyslexic children, structure and organization are particularly important, and a parenting style that provides loving guidelines is crucial.

# self-esteem boosters

When I was in junior high school, I was the fastest runner in the school. Even when I was criticized by teachers or teased by kids, I had the comeback, "Well, I can run faster than you." It may have seemed a small thing, but to me the fact that I excelled at something made a big difference. Let's look at some of the things that will help your child feel good about herself.

**Help your child experience success.** Let her find a place where she can shine, whether it's sports, the arts, scouting, computer club, or any other venue. Being part of a team is a wonderful way to meet new people, learn about others, and contribute. But make sure your child is having fun and not becoming overly competitive. Sports should be fun; competition will naturally kick in when kids get older. Until grade eight or so, sports should be about playing and having a good time, not about winning.

**Encourage her to volunteer.** Kids who help out at a hospital, nursing home, or charity organization will find that helping others makes them feel good about themselves. A dyslexic child can sing a song to an elderly neighbor, deliver flowers to folks in a nursing home, or take teddy bears to a children's hospital just as well as any kid can. There are plenty of opportunities for children to contribute to their communities, and this is a valuable way for your child to learn that other people also have problems, as well as to boost her own feelings of self-worth. In addition, it shifts her from "receiving" so much special attention from others to giving it. She may find this a welcome relief and satisfying.

**Build skills.** Throughout this book, I've encouraged you to become involved and take an active part in helping your child with schoolwork. But I also want to stress once again that you should help your child with the things that she *can't* do, not with the things that she can. Your child needs to be independent and develop her own capabilities; your role is to guide and support her—not to do things for her. Teach your child to problem-solve (we'll be looking at specific strategies in upcoming chapters). One of the best ways to instill confidence is to give your child the tools to achieve her own success.

**Let your child make decisions.** Yes, you're the parent, but part of being a confident individual is making decisions. We talked about involving your child in goal-setting. You can also give her other opportunities to make decisions and express her opinions. Ask her to help plan the location of your next family outing or to pick the movie you'll see on the weekend. Maybe she can plan and help make the family dinner one night a week. Offering children an opportunity to make choices is an important way to help them feel better about themselves.

**Give your child responsibilities.** Confidence stems from accomplishments, and the dyslexic child may be particularly vulnerable in this area because she struggles academically. Giving your child responsibilities will help build her self-esteem whether her job is to feed and walk the dog or to set the table each night. Knowing that she contributes to the family will help her feel important.

**Offer respect.** Listen to and respect your child. It may seem obvious, but often parents are too rushed or busy to sit down and really pay attention to what their children are saying. The message you give

## Positive Words for Kids

Like adults, kids can fall into the trap of making negative comments about themselves. Help your child convert negative thoughts into positive assertions.

- Instead of "I'm so dumb," try "I'm not dumb; I just have a learning problem."
- Instead of "I can't do this," try "I can do this; I just have to try a new way or take more time."
- Instead of "Why is it so easy for Billy?" say "I can do other things Billy can't do. Everyone has strengths and weaknesses."
- Instead of "My teacher's always yelling; I must be stupid," say "She doesn't know how to deal with dyslexics. I need to talk to somebody about this and get help."
- Instead of "It takes me so much longer than the others," try "I have to work harder, but I know I can get the same results."
- Instead of "I'll never finish," try "I can do it."
- Instead of "It's not fair that I have dyslexia," try "I'm lucky to have great friends and a supportive family."

your child when you are too busy to listen to her is that she is not really that important. Of course, most parents are rushed, and we all live hectic lives, but if you schedule listening and talking time into your day—even if it's just before bedtime or during a family dinner—your child will know that her thoughts and feelings really do matter. This is a powerful self-esteem builder.

**Provide positive self-feedback.** Kids enhance their self-esteem when they learn how to respond to themselves in a positive way when goals are attained. Using phrases such as "I now know I can do this if I start well enough in advance" and "Wow, I did a good job on this assignment!" are examples of positive self-feedback that you can prompt your child to learn and use.

# when self-esteem drops

Kids often exhibit signs of low self-esteem by making negative remarks about themselves. They may also ask for help when they don't really need it or refuse to try new things. A child with low self-esteem may be too easily influenced by his peers, or he may overreact to criticism or minor failures. Self-esteem research shows that successes raise levels of self-assessment, and failures lower these levels. Repeated failures can have devastating effects on self-esteem. When someone has a series of successes, there is greater tolerance for an occasional failure. Here's what you can do.

**Step in to help.** Kim, a second grader, is feeling bad about herself. Her reading, writing, and spelling are poor, and the other kids seem to know that "something is wrong." She has been excluded by a group of girls she hoped were her friends, and though her teacher is helping as much as she can, Kim's self-esteem has taken a major hit. Kim comes home from school crying each day. "I'm so dumb," she tells her mother.

## Ten Common Mistakes Parents of Dyslexic Children Make

There's no doubt that raising a dyslexic child can be challenging, but the job becomes easier when you learn from the mistakes—and successes—of other parents. I've found these to be the 10 most common problem areas that parents of dyslexic kids encounter.

- Thinking that your child will be "normal" someday and his dyslexia will be cured
- Blaming yourself for your child's dyslexia
- Believing you understand exactly what your child is going through
- Failing to understand what your dyslexic child can and can't do
- Helping your dyslexic child with tasks he can do on his own
- Hiding your child's dyslexia from others
- Lowering rather than re-focusing expectations
- Trying to protect your child from the real world
- Fighting with the school system instead of working together
- Focusing on your child's "disabilities" rather than his abilities

In Kim's case, teachers and parents should step in to help. She is young and won't know how to solve the problem on her own. Her teacher or parent could help her to find one buddy who would befriend her. Sometimes, an older child can give support and offer to show her the ropes. Joining an after-school program might also help by providing a group in which to belong and experience success.

**Realize it's not a gift.** Self-esteem is not a gift you can give your child; it's something inside him that develops over time. With your love and support, as well as your help in finding ways to problem-solve and pursue strategies, your dyslexic child will develop a sense of mastery that will last a lifetime.

# 15. Strategies for Success at School

School will be the place where your child's dyslexia is likely to have the most obvious impact. As he reads, writes, completes assignments, and interacts with peers and his teachers, your child will confront his learning disability on a daily, ongoing basis. Supportive parents and teachers, as well as a carefully designed Individualized Education Program (IEP), will help your child to flourish, even in a demanding academic environment. In this chapter, I'll look at some of the tools and strategies available to your child in the school setting. Keep in mind, however, that each dyslexic child has individual needs, so you will need to experiment with the solutions until you find the best fit.

## the key tool: communication

Because you are at home or at work and not in the classroom, you will not always know what your child encounters during the school day.

162

## Tips for Teacher Meetings

The following tips will help you to get the most out of your meetings with your child's teacher.

- Take time before the meeting to talk with your child and find out if he has concerns he would like you to raise.
- Prepare your questions in advance. Jot down a list.
- Bring your spouse or partner, if possible. For an IEP conference, also bring your own expert (a social worker or friend who will be familiar with the terminology being used).
- Arrive on time.
- Be prepared to listen.
- Remain calm and composed, even if you feel riled. If you believe a question isn't being answered well or adequately, rephrase the question or ask for the answer to be rephrased.
- Ask your most important questions first. If you run out of time, request a follow-up meeting in a few weeks and set a time for this meeting before you leave.
- Ask your child's teacher for specific suggestions and examples throughout the meeting.
- Ask what you can do at home to support and foster your child's progress.

However, by keeping the lines of communication open with his teachers and discussing trouble spots and strategies with them, you can work together to find and support your child's best learning style. Remember to keep in close contact with the teacher to ensure that she is implementing methods in the classroom that will aid your child.

- Set up regular check-in meetings with your child's teacher to monitor progress and discuss concerns. Some (but not all) teachers will be willing to meet with you each week or to check in on the phone on a weekly basis.

- Use e-mail to communicate with the teacher when person-to-person meetings or phone calls aren't feasible.
- Volunteer in the classroom when possible. Be a field trip chaperone or volunteer to be the class mom or dad. This will help develop your relationship with the teacher.

# tools for reading

*Annette is a bright fourth grader, but her reading skills lag far behind the rest of her class, due to her dyslexia. At the beginning of the school year, she was struggling daily, but after her teacher, Mr. Nichols, began to implement ideas from her IEP, her reading began to improve. For one thing, Mr. Nichols no longer rushes her when she reads aloud, and sometimes he helps her pronounce the words, standing at her side and softly whispering when she is hesitant. Annette has also found that books on tape have really helped. When the class was reading* Little House on the Prairie, *Annette's mother located an audiotape through the local library's interlibrary loan system, and Annette listened to it every night before she went to bed. Though reading aloud remains a challenge, Annette feels more confident that she will at least be able to understand the story line and grasp the main characters when she reads a book.*

- Ask your child to read the material, reread the material, talk to someone about what she has read, and then read it again.
- If your child is reading a novel or short story, get a copy for yourself and read along so that you will be able to discuss the material with her. Or encourage her to call or get together with a friend to talk about what she has read.
- Leave enough time. Your child will need extra time for reading and rereading the material.
- Let your child read in small doses; schedule frequent breaks.

- Make use of books on tape. Many books already exist on audiotape; check your library or bookstore. At the end of the term or school year, remember to get books your child will need for the next semester so that you can have the audiotapes on hand in time.

- Watch a film of the book. Multisensory materials—materials that make use of sight, touch, and hearing—are important channels for the dyslexic learner.

## Multisensory Materials

Throughout this book, I recommend the use of multisensory materials when possible. Why are they so effective? Children with dyslexia—indeed, all children—learn in different ways, and using multisensory materials provides a variety of opportunities to help your child learn. Imagine that your child's teacher always lectured from a podium. Then imagine how much more effective that teacher would be in reaching your child if he let the students work on hands-on projects, conduct experiments, or go on a field trip.

The idea behind multisensory materials is to suit the individual needs of the child and let him use his senses, especially the senses of touch and hearing. Some kids may learn to spell if they are given a chance to explore writing with a real tactile element. For example, writing with a squeeze-style mustard bottle, shaving cream, or hair gel or writing with your finger, using trays of colored sand or salt, may aid the learning process. Another option is to build words with wooden letters, blocks, or puzzle pieces. A projector and sound system can also be used to stimulate learning. Keep in mind, however, that some kids (such as those with ADHD) may find some aspects of this approach to be overstimulating. The key is to make sure the teacher understands what your child needs and adjusts the multisensory materials used to fit his learning style.

- Ask your child to make a list of new characters as she reads. Have her write down pertinent facts about each character and the page number where the character was first introduced.

- Use self-adhesive notes. Your child can use these stickies on various pages to identify important parts of the story and make it easier to go back to them for reference.

- Let your child use a piece of cardboard or a bookmark to block out other lines on the page as she reads. This is particularly helpful for keeping place and reducing distraction.

- Let your child know she can take her time.

## Sample Reading Plan (Grades 4 to 6)

Working closely with your child on his reading assignments is one of the most important ways you can support your child's school success. Here's an example of how you can talk to your child about material he is reading. Guiding him through the text will help him comprehend and enjoy the story.

*On nearer approach he was still more surprised at the singularity of the stranger's appearance. He was a short, square-built old fellow, with thick bushy hair, and a grizzled beard. His dress was of the antique Dutch fashion—a cloth jerkin strapped round the waist—several pair of breeches, the outer one of ample volume, decorated with rows of buttons down the sides, and punches at the knees. He bore on his shoulder a stout keg, that seemed full of liquor, and made signs for Rip to approach and assist him with the load. Though rather shy and distrustful of his new acquaintance, Rip complied with his usual alacrity; and mutually relieving one another, they clambered up a narrow gully, apparently the dry bed of a mountain torrent. As they ascended, Rip every now and then heard long, rolling peals, like distant thunder, that seemed to issue out of a deep ravine, or rather cleft, between lofty rocks, towards which their ragged path conducted.*

—From *Rip Van Winkle* by Washington Irving

- Before she reads, preview the material with your child. Estimate the time it will take to complete a passage. Schedule a break at a particular point. During the preview, focus on pictures or graphs and discuss them. Anticipate how they will relate to the content.

- If the material has a summary at the end, read it first. This provides an overview and gives a framework for the detailed content.

- Have a brief discussion *before* reading. Anticipate questions about the content. Read to answer these questions, stopping to answer them briefly.

---

**Preview the material.** Prepare your child for the introduction of a new character. You might say, "Rip is about to meet someone new in this section." Provide a highlighter or self-adhesive notes so your child can earmark the place where a new character enters the story.

**Explain the meaning of new words.** Does your child know what "singularity" means? What is a cloth jerkin and breeches? Discuss what the author means by "His dress was of the antique Dutch fashion." Explain any other words that might be confusing to your child. Does he know what a gully is? If not, perhaps you can find a picture in a book or on the computer. What about the word "alacrity"?

**Model comprehension.** Use words to show your child your own understanding of what's going on. "So! Rip is meeting up with a very interesting little man carrying a mysterious load. He must be very surprised to meet this stranger in the woods! Let's read on to see what happens next."

**Discuss the plot and new characters.** "Why do you think Rip is distrustful of this odd fellow? They're helping one another carry their load. Where do you think they are headed? I wonder if something will happen next that will change Rip's life. What do you think that noise is—can you imagine the sound of distant thunder like we heard at the lake last summer?"

*Whether I shall turn out to be the hero of my own life, or whether that station will be held by anybody else, these pages must show. To begin my life with the beginning of my life, I record that I was born (as I have been informed and believe) on a Friday, at twelve o'clock at night. It was remarked that the clock began to strike, and I began to cry, simultaneously.*

*I was born at Blunderstone, in Suffolk, or "thereby" as they say in Scotland. I was a posthumous child. My father's eyes had closed upon the light of this world six months when mine opened on it. There is something strange to me, even now, in the reflection that he never saw me.*

*An aunt of my father's and consequently a great-aunt of mine, of whom I shall have more to relate by-and-by, was the principal magnate of our family; Miss Trotwood, or Miss Betsey, as my poor mother always called her when she sufficiently overcame her dread of this formidable personage to mention her at all (which was seldom).*

—From *David Copperfield* by Charles Dickens

**Preview the material.** What is *David Copperfield* going to be about? Talk about what it means to be an orphan today and what it would have meant in David Copperfield's time. Discuss Charles Dickens and the time in which he lived, 1812 to 1870. What was it like in England during this period? Has your child read or seen *A Christmas Carol*? What other

- If your child has auditory strengths, try having her summarize reading passages in her own words into a tape recorder. This will provide an ongoing summary of the material that can be reviewed on a regular basis.

# time and sequence aids

*Tommy, 13, is not able to keep historical facts in sequence. He has trouble remembering the order of the presidents, and sometimes, he gets confused* resources can you think of to help familiarize your child with Dickensian England?

**Explain the meaning of new words.** Ask your child if he knows what David means when he says the clock and his cry began "simultaneously." What is the meaning of "posthumous"? What does "magnate" mean? Look up the words together if your child does not know the definitions.

**Discuss the point of view of the story.** Make sure your child understands that Dickens has written the story in what is called first person, as if David himself were telling it.

**Discuss characters as they are introduced.** Ask your child if he thinks Miss Betsey will be important to the story. How can the reader tell? What does David mean when he calls his aunt "formidable?" Ask your child what kind of person he thinks Miss Betsey will be. How does David's mother feel about her?

**Model comprehension.** "Hmmm, it's unusual that David's father died just six months before he was born." Or, "Something must happen to his mother, too. I wonder who will raise him."

**Discuss the plot.** "What do you think the narrator means when he says this story will show whether he will be the hero of his own life?" You might ask your child, "Do you think the fact that he is an orphan will have an important impact on what happens to him?"

*about north, south, east, and west. His teacher has created a permanent visual display for the classroom that is useful for all students, especially those with learning disabilities. She has designed a timeline that pictorially charts critical historical events and the presidents. Tommy is doing much better in history this year because his teacher knows that visual clues work better than rote memorization for some kids.*

- Help your child learn facts by hearing rather than reading alone.

- Use multisensory methods—seeing, hearing, touching. Read a book, listen to the book on tape, and then see the movie (such as *Harry Potter and the Sorcerer's Stone*).

- Suggest that the teacher use pictorial wall charts and timelines. If you can, work with your child to develop timelines together. Make it fun by using creative and tactile materials (marshmallows, Day-Glo stickers, and so on) to indicate points in a sequence.

- Use old magazines to select pictures that represent content to be organized into a sequence. Work with your child to construct this. Don't do it for him.

# tools for writing

*Beth is writing a book report for her seventh-grade class. Her teacher gives her the same information as the other students, including clear, written directions. Beth goes over the directions with her mom and maps out a plan. Beth reads the book but also rents the movie version. Then she creates an outline and a timeline for the work. Following her outline, she types her paper into her word processor, then uses the spell-check tool built into the software to make sure there are no mistakes. Her mom double-checks for errors, and Beth makes a few final corrections. She and her mom discuss the book, movie, and paper as Beth makes progress.*

- Make sure the directions for writing assignments are clear; ask your child to talk to her teacher if she is confused.

- Ask your child to restate the directions in her own words for reinforcement and clarification.

- Encourage your child to get help with organization before she begins. If you feel comfortable doing so, help her to make an outline or some organized list of what needs to be done. Don't feel compelled to rely on formal outline presentations. Sometimes, a list works just as well.

- Work together to create a timeline for completion of the work. Break it down into as many steps as you feel necessary.

- If the writing assignment is a book report, as your child reads the book, let her also rent the movie and listen to the audio-tape. Discuss the story together.

- Let your child use a word processor to type the report.

- Remind her to use the spell-checking feature. Remember, however, this feature isn't perfect; if your child means to write "fast" but types "fat" instead, the spell checker won't catch that error. Enlist the help of a parent, tutor, or peer to edit the work and do a "manual" spell check.

- For auditory learners, try having the child construct the report orally and read it into a tape recorder. The oral report can be organized around topics that are developed first. Since writing is "talking written down," the child can then transpose the oral words into written format.

# spelling strategies

*Dean has a lot of trouble with spelling. His dad has discovered that if he arranges the words the boy is trying to learn to spell in a particular order, Dean is much more likely to remember them. Dean's dad talks to the teacher about the kinds of words Dean is learning (he finds that it's easier for Dean to learn common words that he uses on a daily basis) and asks her to arrange the words in a logical sequence. Before long, Dean's spelling grades are improving. He is able to remember more words because of the memory clues. Dean also has a "spelling box"—his dad places pictures representing the words in a box, and Dean goes over these before the test. His teacher keeps a similar box for him at school.*

- Let your child's teacher know spelling presents a particular problem for your child.

- Request that your child receive two grades on written essays—one for spelling and one for content.
- Arrange spelling lists in order—by subject matter or by similar prefixes, for instance.
- Create a spelling box: Cut out pictures from magazines that represent the words your child must learn. Label the pictures and ask your child to review the pictures and words daily. This will provide visual clues that help prompt memory recall. There is not really a strategy for words that don't have pictures, although you can improvise the best you can. For instance, use an actual syllabus to illustrate the word *syllabus* or use an actual calendar to convey the concept of *yesterday*.

## Creating a Spelling Box

The object of a spelling box is to trigger memory cues so that your child will have less difficulty recalling the spelling of words. If, for instance, your child must learn to spell the word "ball," it will help to let him hold a ball with the word "ball" taped to it. When he encounters this word on a spelling test, he'll be more likely to picture the ball and spell the word correctly. Learning how to spell the word may be easier if he has a visual and sensory cue.

To create a spelling box, take your child's spelling words and find pictures or objects that correspond to them. Work together with your child on this activity, using magazines or props. Make it fun. Don't rush. Place the materials that you've chosen together in a box with plenty of room and review them at regular intervals, such as every other day. Let your child take the pictures out and study them, and encourage him to touch any objects you've included with their spelling attached, such as a ball, paper, glue, hat, and so on. Although spelling each word represented in the box may be difficult for your child, let him spend more time with the words that are most worrisome. Touching, holding, and looking at the words will pique your child's memory.

- Use the sense of touch. Ask your child to trace spelling words in sand sprinkled in a tray. Or have your child form letters from clay, let them dry, and then use the clay letters to construct templates of the words to be spelled. The words can be placed on cardboard and kept in a box to be used again and again.
- Ask your child to write spelling words in the air.
- Use different-colored markers for frequently misspelled parts of words, such as the *ei* in their and the *ere* in there.
- Accept that spelling errors may always be part of your child's writing and encourage the use of a spell checker as much as possible.
- Keep a list of words your child misspells frequently and include them in your child's spelling box. For example, here's a partial list of words I repeatedly spell wrong.

| | |
|---|---|
| Country/countrey | Strategies/stragies |
| County/conty | Surprise/suprize |
| Daughter/dauther | Yesterday/yestarday |
| Dyslexic/dyslexick | Many of the months of the year |
| Embarrassed/embarased | Most cities, states, and countries |
| Foreign/forien | Most proper names |
| Stomach/stomack | |

# tools for math

*Inez, like many dyslexic kids, has trouble with math. The signs for plus, minus, multiplication, and division are confusing. She often arrives at the wrong answers because her columns become misaligned on the page and she adds the wrong digits. Her teacher provided Inez with special graph paper so that she can align the numbers within a grid. Immediately, Inez's grades improved, because her teacher discovered a way to help her stay visually organized.*

- Have your child use a calculator to double-check math problems. A calculator with a print function is even better because it provides two modalities—seeing and touching.
- Practice math drills in small doses—one 15-minute session per day.
- Master small groups of facts at a time; for example, five or six sets of numbers. Don't overwhelm your child with too much information at one time.
- Pair math facts such as 4 + 5 and 5 + 4; 6 + 2 and 2 + 6. Teach backward and forward to make facts easier to grasp.
- Multisensory math learning is best. Whenever possible, use manipulatives (learning materials you use with your hands such as marbles or coins) and games, which help learning. Contact the education-materials company your child's teacher recommends to purchase manipulatives that you and your child can use at home.
- Use grids to align number columns.
- Recheck answers.
- Focus on conceptual understanding, not just rote memorization. Using manipulatives helps develop conceptual understanding and is more effective than a flash card, for instance.
- When your child is faced with word problems, help her break the task into small parts. Start with simple problems and progress slowly.
- Develop your child's confidence by practicing many computational exercises repeatedly.

## taking tests

*Bret is a 13-year-old who has trouble taking tests. When given enough time and help, he can do quite well, and fortunately, his teachers at the middle school are attuned to the fact that Bret needs a different setup than his peers. His English teacher often lets Bret take the exams orally—she writes down his answers as he speaks. Today, she is experimenting with the entire class. On test day, she's allowing the kids to bring in one page filled with information (she calls it the "One Page Wonder"). The students fill the paper with as many facts and details as they can and use this while they are taking the exam. This doesn't just help them during the test—the process of filling out the page is a learning experience. Because of the advance preparation, Bret will do well on this exam.*

- Ask the teacher if your child can be given extra time to complete the test. This is commonly done and not considered exceptional.

## The High Stakes of Testing

Testing is a critical issue for students with learning disabilities. As our society moves more and more into "teaching for the test" and a psychometric approach to intelligence, we need to ensure that the rights of dyslexic and other learning-disabled students are upheld. As your child's advocate, you may find that the responsibility rests on your shoulders for making sure the proper accommodations are made for your child when tests are given.

Often, it's assumed that giving a child more time will solve the issue, but that's not always the case. A dyslexic child may need to have the test read aloud, require a calculator or a dictionary, or need help filling in the answer circles. Because more and more schools are instituting grade-level tests and exit exams that can pose problems for children with dyslexia, keep in close contact with your child's school to guarantee that accommodations are made. When your child is diagnosed with a learning disability, make sure the compensations she needs for standardized testing are recorded in her IEP. Press to ensure that all accommodation options are carefully examined and chosen—your child may need more than just "more time."

- Inquire if at least part of the test can be oral rather than written.

- If it's a math test, ask if your child can use a calculator.

- Ask if the test can be administered as a take-home exam.

- Make sure your child is well-rested and has eaten breakfast before the test.

- Ask the teacher to provide a study guide before the test or work with your child to prepare one together.

- Remind your child to ask the teacher for clarification if he does not understand any test direction.

- Inquire how long the test will take and if your child can take a short break if it is lengthy.

- Inquire about mastery learning, in which the teacher administers the test, corrects it, and allows the student to take the test again for a better grade.

- Remember that not all teachers will be willing to make adjustments for tests; request that the teacher carefully follow your child's IEP.

- Tests should be viewed as opportunities for learning and not as rewards or punishment. Review graded tests with your child and discover the reasons for wrong answers.

- Take simulated tests at home. This helps build confidence and reduces anxiety.

# taking notes

*Jasmine has trouble listening and writing at the same time. When she focuses on the teacher, she misses notes in class. When she focuses on taking notes, she can't pay attention to what the teacher is saying. In science, taking notes is an important part of class, so she talks to the teacher about what she can do. Mr. Hughes agrees that Jasmine can bring a tape recorder to class, or if she prefers, Mr. Hughes will provide her with a copy of his own notes to use at home.*

- Ask if your child can bring a tape recorder, PalmPilot–type device, or laptop to class for note-taking.

- Ask the teacher if a peer can take notes for your child. Or inquire if the teacher can give your child her notes or provide a guide he can follow to aid in note-taking. A topic guide for note-taking is an excellent way to make the task more focused and organized.

- Ask if a friend will let your child photocopy his notes. This is a common and acceptable practice used by students who are learning disabled.

- Buy erasable pens and writing utensils with pencil grips. Erasable pens help your child correct his mistakes neatly, avoiding self-esteem issues that can arise when papers are unsightly. Pencil grips are helpful for kids who have difficulty with fine motor skills.

- If the dyslexic child takes his own notes, ask the teacher to review his notebook to make sure the information is correct and all pertinent material is included.

- Make sure your child sits in the front of the class near the chalkboard if he is taking his own notes.

- Use a loose-leaf three-ring binder notebook rather than a spiral notebook. Papers can be inserted later if additional notes need to be slipped in.

- Consider using paper that has very wide lines for ease of writing and reading later.

- Work with your child to review and organize notes after they are written.

- Writing key words in the margins of notes after they are taken is a helpful way to review and remember content.
- Have your child type his handwritten notes into the computer at home to help reinforce the information. Print out a copy and put it in his loose-leaf notebook. This helps your child feel assured that his notes are neat as well.

# following directions

*Carmen seems to be listening intently when her teacher gives the directions for the history test, but when the other students start writing, she is still staring at her paper. Mrs. Nugent is aware that Carmen has problems with listening skills, so she approaches her desk and quietly asks her to repeat the directions back to her. Sure enough, she has confused the directions and isn't sure how to do the fill-in-the-blanks section. Mrs. Nugent explains once again that all the words needed for the blanks can be found in the upper right-hand box. She suggests that Carmen cross out each word she uses with her pencil as she goes along.*

- Ask the teacher to double-check with your child to make sure she understands spoken directions.
- Make arrangements with the teacher to have your child repeat the directions back to him.
- If your child is to copy directions from the board, ask the teacher to make sure your child has written them down correctly.
- Ask if the teacher will write the directions in your child's assignment book.
- Make sure your child sits in the front of the class, away from the window.

- Ask the teacher to be sure your child is paying attention. She can use the reminder, "I want your eyes to be looking at my eyes."

- Remind your child that she can ask the teacher for help.

- Use colors to help focus on the sequence of directions. For example, use green to begin, yellow to pause, and red to stop.

# organizing the desk

*Derrick is a dedicated student, but he has serious problems with organizational skills. He never seems to know where he has put anything. At back-to-school night, his mom opens his desk and is horrified to find that it looks like a trash bin inside. Although back-to-school night is not for addressing individual students' problems, she approaches the teacher and asks if they can have a conference soon to discuss Derrick's organizational problems and figure out a way to help him better arrange his desk. The teacher agrees to meet with Derrick's mom the very next day.*

- Work with the teacher to designate a weekly time for your child to organize his desk—after school on Fridays, for instance, or Monday before school starts.

- Take a Polaroid picture of the way the inside of the desk should look and tape it to the underside of the desk or to your child's notebook. Organization is crucial for dyslexic kids.

- Explain to your child that books should be arranged in the same order each week, so that he will be able to easily find a book when he needs it.

- Use colored book jackets to provide visual clues—green for science, red for reading—but also clearly write the subjects on the covers. Using color makes the process of organizing

## Color-Coding

I often recommend the use of color-coding as an aid to learning for children with dyslexia. Why does this seem to work so well? Many children with learning disabilities are visual learners. Using color helps these kids make visual associations that prompt learning and memory. For instance, when your child highlights his reading materials with a colored highlighter or marks in yellow each time a new character appears in the text of a story or novel, the learning process becomes more active. Using different colors for different tasks helps your child sort out and recall the information.

There are many ways to employ color-coding. Be creative! When I wrote my dissertation, I color-coded my research materials and also used colored paper tabs to differentiate related topics. Color-coding your child's appointment book or calendar can also be useful: hockey in green, basketball in blue, music lessons in red; or, science assignments in green, social studies in yellow. Let your child choose his own colors—he may already have established associations with a particular color that will help him remember. Color-coded maps can also be useful to the dyslexic child.

anything more visual and less word-dependent for the dyslexic child. He will see green and think science more readily than he can read the word "science" on the book cover and process its meaning. The color modality (way of learning) is much stronger than the word modality for dyslexics.

- Provide a plastic case for pencils, pens, glue sticks, and other materials.

- Keep materials for each subject separate and use colored files or notebooks for each different subject.

# getting work in on time

*Jeb has a problem remembering when his assignments are due. He writes the dates down in his notebook, but he never seems to hand his papers in on time. His teacher suggests that he keep a goal chart at school as well as at home, so he can chart his progress on assignments. She agrees to meet with Jeb after school to help him fill in the dates and times that various assignments are due. At home, his mother will check off the dates when Jeb has completed each step of the assignments.*

- Ask your child to talk to his teacher about how he can get his work in on time.

- Encourage your child to create goal charts (see chapter 11).

- Ask your child's teacher to give him plenty of advance notice when an assignment is due. Explain that he will need extra time to complete the task and plan his strategies.

- At home, provide a large laminated calendar with erasable markers. On the calendar, post all assignments for the month. Post not only when they are due but also when work on an assignment will begin. Every morning or evening, check the calendar, review, and make any necessary revisions.

- Work with your child to plan to complete assignments before the due date, if possible. This provides opportunities for revision and refinement.

- Develop strategies for completing assignments at the last minute. This is a reality, and it helps to have a plan for getting things done quickly.

- At first, extrinsic rewards (stars, special privileges) for completing work on time may be helpful. Later, the reward will be finishing the work itself.

# navigating classroom changes

*Carrie, 14, has just entered ninth grade at the high school. This is the first year she will start changing classrooms for each class. She is terrified that she will become lost on the first day of school and not be able to find her way in the building, which is so much larger than the middle school she attended last year. Although her best friend, Sadie, is in most of her classes and Carrie can usually walk with her there, she can't always depend on her. What if Sadie is out sick, or what if Carrie needs to talk to the teacher after class and doesn't leave at the exact same moment as Sadie?*

- Remind your child that she can follow or walk with a friend to class.

- Create a backup map. Use color-coded arrows to map your child's path throughout the school: Green goes to the gym, red to English class, yellow goes to history. As with book covers, the dyslexic child responds more quickly to a color association than a word association. Tape the map inside your child's notebook so she can refer to it as she walks.

- If your middle-school or high-school child has block scheduling, in which one schedule (or class sequence) is used for Mondays, Wednesdays, and Fridays with a different schedule for Tuesdays and Thursdays, your child may wish to wear a shirt or sweater in one color, say blue, for Block 1 days and another color, say green, for Block 2 days. To keep wardrobe options even more open, you might try a solid top for Block 1 days and any patterned top for Block 2 days. I know kids for whom this approach works very well.

- Remind your child that it's okay to ask for help.

- Provide alternative strategies. For some students, mobile phones may help in dire situations. Check with your school to see if this is permissible. Make sure your child knows where the school pay phone is located.

# dealing with peers

*Jayne is embarrassed because she sits next to two of the most popular girls in school; they are also two of the brightest students. They know Jayne has a learning disability, but they don't really understand what that means. Each day, they giggle when they get their papers back. They don't mean to be rude, but they can't help noticing the red marks on Jayne's papers.*

- Encourage your child to be honest about her learning disability. Give her the language to use with friends, acquaintances, and even strangers. (For instance, she can say, "I have a learning disability called dyslexia. It means that I learn differently than you, and sometimes I have trouble with reading and spelling.")

- Ask the teacher to seat your child near a friend or near another student who will be positive and supportive.

- Suggest that the teacher give feedback privately, not in front of others. All students benefit from private feedback.

# teacher tactics

*Ashley has four different teachers in middle school, and each one reacts differently to her dyslexia. Mr. Drew is more than willing to give her extra time and extra help, but Mrs. Cooper seems annoyed whenever Ashley asks for clarification. She's beginning to figure out that every teacher is different, and some will be more willing to help than others.*

- You are your child's best advocate; ask to meet with the teacher if you suspect a problem.

- Contact your special services department if you suspect a teacher is not adhering to your child's IEP.

- Let the teacher know what your child's weaknesses—and strengths—are.

- Remember that most teachers want what is best for your child.

- Be proactive. Don't wait for problems to emerge. Meet with the teacher at the beginning of the term and continue to have regular communication.

- Always begin with the teacher first before going to administrators or supervisors over the teacher's head.

# your child can do well in school

Learning is a shared responsibility; the learner, the parent, the teacher, and the administrator all have important roles to play in the education of your child. It's your child's job to do his best, your job to give him the support and tools he needs, the teacher's role to educate and challenge your child, and the special services team's responsibility to make sure that the IEP is properly developed and followed.

Flexibility and backup plans are important. Providing alternate strategies and approaches before problems arise is a key to success in school. If a method isn't effective, communicate with your child's teacher and experiment with alternate strategies. Don't hopelessly say, "It's not working." Say with purpose, "This doesn't work. What can we try next?"

Most importantly, successful learning occurs when learners feel good about themselves, not when they are treated in an overly critical way or devalued. The saying "We learn from our mistakes" goes only so far. Children really learn best when they have a series of successful experiences that form the foundation for growth and development. Work with your child's school to make sure that she is given an opportunity to master small steps along the way and to experience the joy of achievement. Working with the school for a positive outcome is one of the most important things you can do to support your dyslexic child.

# college and your dyslexic child

Going to college can be a daunting prospect even when a child doesn't have dyslexia. If higher education is important to you and your child, you might very well be thinking, "How can I help prepare my child for the multifaceted effort of getting into college?" Consider college a goal you prepare for from day one, and the first step is offering your support and encouragement and guiding your child toward independence. That said, here are some of the practical steps to consider as the college years grow closer.

## Monitor High School Course Requirements

If college is your child's dream, then you must inform her high school guidance counselors early on that this is a goal she is striving for. Sometimes, learning-disabled students are steered away from college preparatory programs. When your child makes up her course schedule, be sure to let her know that she must tell her counselors that college is a priority for her. (Making a phone call to the counselor yourself might also be a good idea.) Otherwise, your child may be pointed toward a course selection that will eventually disqualify her from admission to a 4-year college program.

## Assist in Completing College Applications

Completing college applications can be a complicated process, and your child will most likely need your help. Keep track of when applications are due and make a timeline or a chart to monitor your child's progress toward completion. Allow plenty of time for writing, rewriting, and editing the application essay. Be sure that your child includes detailed information about his extracurricular activities as well as academic achievements. Colleges are increasingly looking at the "whole" student and want to know whether your child has volunteered for community service, joined clubs, played in the school band, and so on. A well-rounded student will be an asset to the college community, so if your child has strengths in areas other than academics, now is the time to play those cards.

## Stay on Top of Testing

Learning-disabled college applicants are not exempt from taking the SATs or ACTs, but your child can receive special accommodations (commonly, more time). It's important to inform the guidance department at your child's high school early (certainly, no later than February or March of junior year) so that any special arrangements for these tests can be made.

Most, if not all, colleges will also require a psychoeducational report completed within the last 1 to 3 years. This is basically the same kind of report that was done when your child was first diagnosed with a learning disability and received an IEP. Some colleges also require the WAIS-R (Wechsler Adult Intelligence Scale-Revised), so check with the guidance department to see when the school psychologist can administer this test.

## Work Closely with the Guidance Department

Keep in close contact with your child's high school guidance department. You may feel like you're being a pest, but that's your job. It's a guidance counselor's job to work to help children like yours, and it's your right and responsibility to be your child's advocate. Do not feel guilty. Don't be shy. As I said earlier, the college application process is a complicated, stressful procedure for kids without learning disabilities; students who have the added concern of dyslexia need plenty of help and guidance to maneuver this path. Rest assured, however, that it *can* be done. There has been no better time for learning disabled kids to go to college than now—the pendulum is truly swinging toward the realization that with the right support, many LD students can and do go on to succeed in academic settings and pursue challenging careers.

## Check Out College Programs

All colleges are legally obligated to offer special services for learning disabled students, but exactly what that means varies from college to college. Some kids may do well with a minimal amount of extra help, but it's imperative to know how much assistance your child will need. If you feel that your child needs an average or maximum amount of assistance, you want to opt for a "comprehensive" program. This means that the college is really geared toward helping learning disabled students. The comprehensive program may include a learning center with full-time, trained staff members, remediation specialists, tutors, counselors, summer programs for LD students, academic advising provided by specially trained staff members, basic skills remediation, campus support groups, and other services. There are many 2-year and 4-year colleges that offer comprehensive programs, and they can be found virtually all over the country. It's essential to research the details, which may vary dramatically from school to school. For example, some colleges allow LD students to take a lighter course load. On the other hand, some may charge an additional fee for special services (ranging from several hundred to several thousand dollars).

The second option is a 2- or 4-year college with special services. What this means will vary from school to school, so research your choices well. The special services department may consist of one person whose time is spread very thin, or it may be comprised of an excellent group of highly qualified remediation specialists and tutors.

The key is finding the best match possible between your child's needs and what the college offers. After gathering information from the guidance counselor at your child's school and other resources, call the colleges your child is seriously considering and ask the LD Program Coordinator any further questions you may have.

## Visit the School

Visiting the campus is a must for any prospective college student, but you will have the added incentive of wanting to see for yourselves exactly what the college has to offer its learning-disabled students. Ascertain how many advisors are available for LD students, what the learning center is like (if there is one), and whether there are adequate computers and other materials for LD students. Ask what other kinds of accommodations are made for LD students. Talk to college personnel and the LD coordinator. At Oakton Community College in Des Plaines, Illinois, where I teach, we offer a variety of assistance to students in the Instruction Supports Service Center. The individuals who work there always steer the students with dyslexia toward my psychology course because they know I will work closely with them.

Another good idea is to ask if you may speak with a few LD students themselves to get a real feel for life on campus and the kind of support offered. Consider the size of the classes, the atmosphere—for example, is it a city or rural campus—and the opportunities for social interaction. Are LD students allowed to tape lectures? Are student note-takers available? (Some colleges actually provide learning disabled kids with notes taken by other students who are proficient in this area.) What is the procedure for obtaining textbooks on tape? What about the faculty? Are they supportive of LD students? What accommodations do they make for tests and quizzes—more time, a reduced distraction environment, use of a word processor? There's a lot to consider! Take lots of notes on your visit. Immediately after each visit, while the experience is still fresh in your minds, make a list of pros and cons and narrow your choices.

## Make a Good Match

Don't forget that the most important thing is to find a college that will be a good match for your child. Certainly, you can steer him in the right direction and arm him with as many facts as you can, but ultimately, the decision is up to him. He has to feel comfortable at the college of his choice. If you have been offering love and support, buoying his support system, and teaching goal-setting all along, he is certain to find a college that will be compatible with his needs and goals. There are many excellent choices.

Be realistic; if you know your child is going to require a good deal of help and guidance to make this work, then steer him toward a college that offers a comprehensive program. If your child has made great strides and requires less and less assistance with each year of high school, then he may want to opt for a college that offers special services. Other options do exist: Some kids go to community college for 2 years, prove that they can do it, and then transfer to a 4-year college. The bottom line is that the right college is waiting for your child; your job is to help him find it!

## Resources for the College-Bound Child with Dyslexia

I can't emphasize enough the importance of thoroughly researching potential colleges. Cultivate your relationship with your child's guidance counselor, research colleges on the Internet, talk to other parents who have gone through the process, and attend college fairs with your child. There are several good books that will help you along the way: *Peterson's Colleges with Programs for Students with Learning Disabilities or Attention Deficit Disorders* and *Colleges That Change Lives: 40 Schools You Should Know About Even If You're Not a Straight-A Student* by Loren Pope are good places to start your search. Be sure to involve your child; this decision is about his or her future.

# 16. Strategies for Success at Home

**Although school is the place** where children with dyslexia most directly experience the impact of their disability, the home environment can make a crucial difference not only in how well your child does in school but also in how comfortably he deals with his disability in daily life. Throughout this book, I've emphasized the importance of a parent's love and care; home is the place where you can really show your child your emotional support.

At home, there are also practical steps you can take to make your child's life run more smoothly and efficiently. In this chapter, I'll talk about simple steps you can take to show your support in practical ways that will make his days run more smoothly and efficiently, and I'll address the ways in which you can provide your child with a strong, caring home base for managing and succeeding with dyslexia.

# dealing with the morning routine

*Nine-year old Virginia dawdles in the morning. She can't seem to keep on track and often ends up late for school. She often forgets to brush her teeth or comb her hair and may set out without her backpack. Virginia's mom, Sylvia, has talked with her daughter's teacher about her problem, and she decides to use a technique that Virginia's teacher uses in school. Sylvia helps Virginia make a series of posters to place in order on the wall in Virginia's room. They depict Virginia's morning routine; each small poster shows a picture of a girl turning off her alarm clock, going into the bathroom, combing her hair, getting dressed, and so on. Together, Virginia and her mom cut out the pictures and paste them on the poster board, and then they place them strategically on the wall so Virginia will see them each morning. Virginia follows the posters to help her keep on track.*

- Use pictorial charts and posters to help your child follow daily routines.

- Place short notes (you might try self-adhesive notes) on the bathroom mirror, on a chalkboard, or on a bulletin board to reinforce daily routines.

- Provide a digital clock in addition to an analog clock; it may be easier for your child to read, and she may be less likely to make a mistake.

- Make a poster or wall chart with the day's routine posted.

- Use color coding to help your child stay organized. For example, make a chart and post basketball games in green, swim meets in red, scout meetings in blue, and so on (you might try purchasing self-adhesive notes in different colors or using sticker dots). As I explained in chapter 15, using color makes the process of organizing anything more visual and less word-dependent for the dyslexic child. The child will see pink and think "swim meet" more readily than he can read the words "swim meet" on the chart and process their meaning. However, do also write the words for each activity. Use both color and words.

- Lay clothes out the night before and make any other necessary preparations for the next day. For example, ask your child to place her science project next to her backpack or have her remember to pack the cookies to take to the scout meeting she'll attend after school.

# fostering good sleep habits

*Darcy was up till midnight watching a movie, so his morning routine is not going well. He forgets to pack his math book and arrives at school a few minutes late. The spelling test is this morning, and though he studied a few days ago, he already knows he's forgotten most of the words. When his teacher asks where his late pass is, he just shrugs; he can't remember where he put it.*

- Sleep is crucial for all kids, but especially so for the dyslexic child. Establish a reasonable bedtime hour and help your child stick to it.

- If the bedtime hour gets out of hand, try gradually moving it forward in 15-minute intervals over the period of a week or two. This may be easier for your child to accomplish than going to bed a half-hour or hour earlier.

- If possible, encourage your child to get his homework done after school (either at home with you or at his after-school program—many such programs provide a quiet corner and help from caregivers). That way, evening hours can be spent in a more relaxed manner, and bedtime can be early. Some

## Being a Patient Parent

When a dyslexic child needs a lot of help with homework or is cranky after staying up too late at night, it's easy to lose patience. But remember, your dyslexic child did not choose to have a learning disability, and he's not being difficult just to drive you nuts! Patience is a virtue, but for parents, it's a necessity as well. For you, the parent of a dyslexic child, patience is an essential key to successfully helping your child every day and over the long term.

Use whatever strategies you can to maintain your patience. Take a break, treat yourself to a slice of cheesecake (but only one!), exercise, have your spouse take over for a while or take turns helping your child, or call a friend and chat for a few moments. You need breaks, too. Working with your child at the public library is a great tactic—you will each be less likely to act out your frustration in public.

When you lose your patience, buy yourself time—then use that time to calm down, regroup, and reflect. How might you have reacted differently and more effectively or productively? What other choices could you have made with your words, expressions, suggestions, or actions? How could you have changed the outcome of the situation? Finally, forgive yourself—after all, it's impossible to be patient all the time—but vow to do better next time. If you've made a choice you're not happy about, tell your child, too. It's not harmful for children to know that grown-ups get frustrated and make mistakes, too. They need to learn that this is only human. The mutual—and verbalized—commitment between parent and child to keep trying and to try new tactics is a wonderful relationship-builder.

children, however, need a break from schoolwork when they get home and do best starting their homework after dinner.

- Try to keep to an evening routine for your child; for example, homework, half-hour of computer or TV time, reading and talking, bathing, and bed. Dyslexic children do best when they follow a routine and know what to expect.

- In situations in which bedtime must be delayed, be patient with your child the next day. Depending on the child's age, you might write a note to give the teacher a "heads up."

- Save important tasks until your child is well-rested; know the best time to do things. For example, if your child didn't get enough sleep, don't expect him to complete his book report after school or sit down to work on that essay he owes his teacher.

- Flex a bit on the weekend, if your child is able to sleep in.

# providing a good work space

*Annie's organizational skills are sorely lacking. Clothing is scattered around her room, and her desk at home is strewn with papers. She sits in front of the TV and works on her math problems, but she doesn't seem to be getting anywhere. Her mom will be home from work in an hour and will want to know why Annie has wasted so much time.*

- Provide a quiet work space for homework, preferably not near a window. Use only this space for schoolwork.

- Provide proper lighting and supplies.

- Make sure the work space is comfortable and that the desk and chair fit the child's size.

- Minimize or eliminate distractions such as the TV and telephone.

- If possible, create a work space for the computer outside the child's room, in a quiet area that is accessible to both her and you.

- Require your child to leave the space neat after each use.

# helping with homework

*Travis expects his mom to sit with him and help him do his homework. But in Travis's case, Mom is doing way too much. Sometimes, she actually completes all the answers, and Travis just copies them onto the page. He has come to depend on his mom and can't sit down to do his homework without her.*

## How to Find a Good Tutor

How can you make sure that you find the right tutor for your child? You can ask friends, teachers, the school psychologist, guidance counselor, or administrator, your community health center, your physician, or the local university for referrals. Ask a potential tutor for references, then check with others who have used the tutor to find out more about his or her personality, teaching style, and effectiveness.

Next, interview the tutor. Ask about the amount of experience she or he has working with children who have learning disabilities and the length of time employed as a tutor. Inquire about other experiences related to tutoring, such as classroom teaching or counseling, and his or her approach to interacting with parents and teachers. You will also want to know how the tutor assesses the student's progress: Are regular assessments made? How often? What form do the assessments take? Reports? Meetings with parents?

If possible, you and your spouse or partner should be involved in the interviewing and selection process. Involve your child in the selection of the tutor as well. Include your child at the interview, and (depending on her age) consider letting her meet with the tutor without you before making a decision. After all, your child will be meeting with this person on a regular basis; she needs to feel comfortable about the choice.

You will also want to ask the tutor about the strategies she uses to boost a student's motivation and self-esteem. How does the tutor use

- Don't "do it for him." Your job is to be a supportive helper, not the worker bee, and to make sure your child has the tools he needs to do his best.

- Focus your help on your child's weaknesses; don't help when he doesn't need it. If your child is good at math, take a step back and allow him to experience success on his own.

the Individualized Education Program (IEP)? Discuss your goals together and make sure that you're on the same page. Make your expectations clear at the outset. What kind of results are you seeking? Can the tutor provide them? It's a good idea to hire the tutor on a trial basis and meet to review progress after a predetermined number of sessions.

Sometimes, tutors work with children in groups. This is an option to consider if you know other children with similar disabilities. This approach may reduce the cost, and your child may learn from the other kids as well. The downside is that your child will not have the benefit of an exclusive, one-on-one learning situation.

After selecting a tutor, make sure you receive the regular progress assessments you had agreed upon at the outset. You should also get regular progress reports from your child's teacher. Ask the tutor to provide you with tutoring session plans on a regular basis so you are aware of progress made during the sessions.

Maintain a balance between involvement and separation. Stay involved to the degree that you know what is happening in tutoring, but remain separate enough not to interfere with the process and to allow the tutor/student relationship to develop in a trusting and supportive way. Tutoring is a two-way street, so make sure your child is on time for sessions and help him follow through on assignments.

- Set reasonable expectations. Don't expect your child to do too much at once or to accomplish a task on the first try.

- Work in small spurts. Let your child take frequent breaks if he needs them. However, if he's working at a good pace and is comfortable, let him stay on task.

- Be sensitive to your child's learning rhythms. Some kids need a break after school before they start their homework. Others do best if they get the homework done right away. Experiment and find out when and how your child works best. Then establish a homework routine your child can follow daily.

- If your child is stuck on a word and calls out for help, spell the word for him. This is not the time to say, "Go look it up in the dictionary."

- Gradually reduce your help over time if your child is making strides.

- Provide different-colored bins for each subject area. In this way, homework for each subject can be organized separately according to color (making it less word dependent).

- Check to see if your school has a homework phone number so your child can check his assignments. See if it offers on-line tutoring help.

- Consider hiring a tutor to help with problem areas.

# managing frustration

*June dreads helping her son, Miguel, with his homework after school. He is often angry and frustrated after repeated attempts and ends up kicking the table or ripping up his papers. Homework time has become a power struggle, with June standing over her son like a policewoman. Miguel often bursts out of the room in anger or tears.*

- Work in short spurts; allow breaks for physical activity or snacks.

- Help your child stay organized; write out a study schedule in advance.

- If a problem recurs, change the routine. If your child faces the same problem over and over again, it's time to change either the work time or the work method.

- Invite a friend over to do homework; your child may modify his behavior when a peer is working nearby.

- Ask the parent of your child's friend if he can go to her house a few days a week after school. Another parent may occasionally have better success or more patience with your child. You can reciprocate in another way—take the kids to the movies or out to a park on the weekend or have the kids to your house for homework another day. Or alternate homework days—one day at a friend's house, another at yours.

- Don't set timers or time limits.

# stocking up on supplies

*Christopher, a fifth grader, often forgets to bring the proper books home after school. Even though his teacher clearly writes the assignments on the board, Christopher may very well neglect to pack the proper books unless she actually checks his backpack for him. Sometimes, the teacher is just too busy, and Christopher's mom ends up driving him back to the school so he can pick up the book he's forgotten.*

- Keep an extra set of texts and workbooks at home. The school may provide a set for you, or you may have to purchase them. This is a backup system; your child will still be required to bring his books home. But if he forgets, you will not have to go out for them or, worse, have an argument with your child.

- Consider purchasing a small home photocopier to make copies of workbooks for backup and studying. If your child does some of the copying himself, this becomes a learning tool as well.

- Have your child keep a pad of self-adhesive notes on his desk at school to write down, through the day, the names of the books he will need to bring home each day.

- If your child is an auditory learner, try having him use a small handheld tape recorder to tape reminders that he will

## The Auditory Learner

How do you know if your child is an auditory learner? If you've observed that your child learns better through tapes, songs, stories, and discussion than through visual reception of information, chances are he is an auditory learner. While we all use three major learning styles—auditory, visual, and kinesthetic—to some degree, many individuals do best with one style or another. Here are some methods you can use at home if your child is an auditory learner.

- Give directions verbally and ask your child to repeat them.
- Use tape recorders for homework assignments. Ask your child's teacher if your child can sometimes complete assignments orally instead of in writing to maximize your child's strengths and reduce frustration.
- For written assignments, have your child first express her thoughts verbally and tape-record her ideas before writing them. Use the tape as a stimulus for writing.
- Find time to discuss homework and make a plan you discuss verbally. Don't depend on writing out to-do lists. Instead, frequently ask your child to repeat the steps or tasks he needs to complete; this will help to reinforce strong auditory memory skills.

listen to at the end of each school day before going home. Ideally, your child will record the reminders himself daily.

# packing the book bag

*Jenny's books and papers are scattered all over the house. Sometimes, she misses her school bus because she can't find a book to place in her backpack. Her mom tries to encourage her to pack the bag the night before, but Jenny often forgets.*

- Ask your child to summarize ideas verbally or prepare a brief "talk" about the content he's studying. Tape-record the summary and listen to it together for reinforcement.
- Pair your child with another child who also has auditory strengths. Provide opportunities for them to discuss schoolwork and share ideas in conversation.
- Play auditory memory games and keep a progress chart. For example, when learning facts, organize a mini-challenge to see how many items your child can remember and repeat back in sequence.
- If music is not a distraction, see if playing music quietly has a calming influence during study time.
- When material is presented in a visual format, ask your child to explain or discuss it verbally. Obviously, your child's teacher has a mix of children in the class, so she will not always be able to focus on the needs of your auditory learner.
- Encourage oral recitation. One of the most powerful memory devices is reciting out loud; auditory learners should do as much of this as possible.

- Help your child rehearse packing and unpacking her book bag or backpack.
- Ask her to recite the names of the books as she packs them. This is good memory training.
- Pack the bag each night; don't wait until morning.
- Keep the backpack in exactly the same place every night, so that when your child goes out the door in the morning, she will not have to search for it.
- Encourage your child to keep all her school papers and books in one work area until they are ready to be packed.

## getting help from friends

*Clint often confuses dates and times. His mom keeps a calendar by the phone, along with a list of friends he can call for information. Even if she isn't home, Clint knows who to call to find out when soccer practice is. Sometimes, he confuses the date when he looks at the calendar, so he always calls a friend to double-check.*

- Post a list of three to five friends your child can call to verify homework, class trips, or extracurricular events.
- Help your child write thank-you notes to parents, teachers, or friends who help; your child's appreciation will inspire them to help again.

## reading at home

*Beverly's mom has been reading* The Fellowship of the Ring *aloud before bed each night, and 10-year-old Beverly can't wait to see the movie. The book is too hard for her to read herself, but she enjoys listening and sometimes she pitches in by reading a paragraph or two to her mom.*

- Read assigned books with your child. Let her read one paragraph and then you read two. Or perhaps she can read one page and then you read two.

- Explain the meaning of new words.

- As your child reads, stop to discuss what she is learning and explain what is going on in the story.

- Let your child's teacher know how much time she spends on reading assignments. Some teachers may shorten assignments based on the length of time your child can handle comfortably.

- Read to your child daily.

- Encourage your child to read short newspaper articles; try the arts pages if she likes movies or the sports page if she likes sports.

- Use audiotapes and videotapes as well as books.

- Pursue multisensory avenues. If your child is reading about rocks, take her to a museum where she can see and touch them. If the book is about a fireman, make a visit to your local fire station.

- Use puppets to act out stories for younger children. Encourage your child to participate.

# writing at home

*Writing is a chore for Seth. His mom wants him to write thank-you notes to the 10 friends who attended his tenth birthday party, but she knows this will be too much for him. She suggests he sit down at the computer and design a note he can send to all the kids.*

- Encourage your child to use a word processor and the spell checker.

## The Kinesthetic Learner

Kinesthetic learners love to get up and move about; hands-on activities such as painting, working with tools, tracing, sky-writing, or keyboarding appeal to their learning style. Sitting in a chair all day reciting facts is definitely not the way to go for any student—but the kinesthetic learner really suffers in that kind of atmosphere. Too often, classroom learning is auditory and visual and doesn't provide enough opportunities for the kinesthetic learner. Talk with the teacher about expanding opportunities for more active, interactive, and relevant activities. Here are some more ideas.

- Find opportunities to go on field trips to introduce or provide additional reinforcement for new information. Suggest field trip ideas to your child's teacher, but be sure to take your child on your own to museums (especially hands-on museums), concerts, the beach, historical sites, nature hikes, and so on to further explore educational concepts that have been introduced in the classroom setting.
- Help your child use a combination of senses to learn new material. For example, when he's learning something new, encourage him to talk about it, write about it, listen to someone else tell about it, and employ a hands-on activity, when possible, to reinforce the concept.
- Whenever possible, relate learning to real-life experiences. Make the information relevant and applicable to what is happening in your child's life. If your child is learning about maps at school, help him make a simple map of your neighborhood or, for an older child, a detailed map of your town. If your child is working on a health or nutrition unit, get into the kitchen and cook together—you might try

- Use a double-dictation method for writing projects at home, such as a letter to Santa, thank-you notes, birthday party lists, and so on. Ask your child to dictate as you write; then have him write as you read the work back.

- Answer your child's requests for help with spelling.

something simple and delicious like a fruit salad or a shake with fresh fruit, orange juice, and yogurt.

- Use role playing to approach new material and to review what has been learned. Take the key concepts in a lesson and find a way to organize them into a real situation that can be simulated in a role play.

- Encourage writing notes as much as possible. Keeping active with a pen or pencil reinforces kinesthetic learners.

- Prepare material that can be manipulated. For example, put content on study cards and divide them into categories for recitation.

- When your child needs to make an oral presentation in class, provide opportunities to make real-life applications or do something relevant and active with the content. For example, if the presentation is on the culture of a particular country, include music, food, or art as part of the activity. Have him tell stories that bring the content to life.

- Let your kinesthetic learner hopscotch, clap his hands, or snap his fingers while reciting or spelling words.

- Talk to your child's teacher about how your child learns best. If possible, volunteer to help with hands-on projects in the classroom. Bring in a rock or seashell collection during a science segment, or your homemade drum collection for a music lesson. Many teachers will be happy to hear your suggestions. Some teachers, however, prefer kids to sit still and listen. If this is the case, do your best to convey your child's needs.

- Provide erasable pens and pencils with grips, which make writing easier and less frustrating.

- Practice writing at home: Ask your child to help you write the grocery list. Or help him compose a letter to a friend or cousin who lives out of state.

If your child needs to "see" what he's learning, chances are he's a visual learner. The spoken word may seem to just "go in one ear and out the other," but if books, charts, movies, colors, drawings, posters, and maps—in short, anything visual—get the message across, then your child is likely a visual learner. If so, you can take advantage of many materials and methods that will help him absorb information effectively. Here are a few ideas.

- Help your child organize material he is learning into charts, graphs, or diagrams. Show examples first to provide models for this activity.
- Encourage your child to use colored markers to organize information. For example, when he's putting ideas or facts into categories, your child can use colors to delineate each grouping.
- Find picture books in the library to illustrate concepts being presented in school texts.
- Have your child prepare large posters to summarize the content she's learning. Hang the posters in her room for frequent review and reinforcement.
- Organize tasks into charts or lists and make these easily accessible. Provide opportunities for your child to mark off the items he has completed and keep a visual record of accomplishments.

# studying for tests

*Mickey and his mom curl up on the couch every Thursday night and study for the week's vocabulary test. After he goes over the words with his mom, Mickey types them into his word processor, then reads the list, rereads it, and reviews it again with his mother.*

- When faced with auditory tasks, encourage your child to take notes; while he listens, he should also make some kind of visual record of the material.
- For in-class presentations, promote the idea of using visual aids. For example, have your child prepare overhead transparencies, posters, or charts to support the material he's presenting.
- Encourage your child to use concept-mapping to organize large amounts of material. Concept-mapping is a strategy that requires summarizing information into key ideas and representing them visually in an organized way on one sheet of paper. For instance, the main idea of a textbook chapter might be placed in the center of a wheel, with spokes emerging from it to represent supporting concepts; a diagram in the style of a family tree shows the main ideas at the top with subordinate ideas in the branches underneath. After creating a concept map, your child can use it to review and reinforce information without relying heavily on rote memorization.
- Visual learners profit from being well-organized. Your child can organize material in different colored folders or binders for each subject. Within each folder or binder, colored tabs can further define categories within each subject. Sometimes adding pictures cut out from magazines and pasted into the folders can help reinforce ideas.
- Look for videotapes or television programs that relate to the material your child is learning.

- Make a plan for studying. Decide in advance exactly what content will be reviewed and how much time will be spent.
- Make recitation part of every study session. The single most important factor in retaining material over time is reciting it aloud.

- Organize, organize, organize. Study sessions that begin with a specific goal are the most successful. "Let's review five facts about the Civil War tonight" rather than "Let's go over the Civil War era."

- Start studying well in advance. Avoid cramming.

- Study from "the top down." It's easier to understand well-organized material. Start with a main idea and work down to the details.

- Avoid new material the night before the exam. Reinforce what your child knows rather than introducing new concepts.

- Help your child write out a topic summary; this can help him recall and remember material.

- Make sure your child gets enough sleep.

# keeping an eye on technology

*Jess, a college freshman, has a new computer with a voice recognition program. He speaks into the computer, and words pop up on the screen. He uses the program to record his notes from class. As a dyslexic, Jess finds that this technology saves him a great deal of time.*

- Keep abreast of new technology.

- Provide your child with electronic tools. Get a computer or a PalmPilot–type device with word processing software, a spell checker, an electronic dictionary and thesaurus, and an appointment calendar. These are invaluable for dyslexic children.

- Consider purchasing a "reading machine." This special type of scanner, originally developed for the blind, allows you to scan a book into the computer, which then "reads" it back to you. See the Resources section at the back of the book for a

Web site with this and other technology. (And speaking of technology, there's also a talking compass. It's great for the dyslexic driver. I do much better with directions now that I have a compass in my car. Although mine doesn't talk, it has a digital readout, which I find very helpful.)

# doing chores

*Arabella's job is to feed her hamster every morning and clean its cage once a week. This is a 10-year-old who takes her chores very seriously. She has posted Spike's daily menu on the refrigerator. She also helps set the table and clear the dishes after dinner each night.*

- Give your child age-appropriate chores so that she knows she is an important member of the family who contributes on an ongoing basis. Contributing to the family helps foster your child's self-esteem.
- Create a chore chart she can follow to keep track of her responsibilities.
- Offer praise for a job well done.

# handling siblings

*Cynthia is a sixth grader with a dyslexic younger brother. Lately, she's been wondering why her parents pay so much attention to Neil and seem to care so little about her. They didn't even make a fuss when she won the school spelling bee. She's beginning to feel as if her accomplishments don't really matter.*

- Emphasize that each child has strengths as well as weaknesses; don't be afraid to praise your non-dyslexic child.
- Talk to your children about dyslexia and how it will affect them.

- Hold family meetings and encourage all members to express their concerns.
- Make time to give individual attention to your non-dyslexic child.

# having fun

*Every Wednesday night, Dominic, who is dyslexic, goes out to dinner with his dad while his mom takes a computer class. Father and son each enjoy their time together and like to try different restaurants. The time alone gives them a chance to talk about Dominic's interests, as well as to plan weekend activities the family can enjoy together, such as hiking or ski trips.*

- Make time for fun, free of heavy discussions.
- Plan time to appreciate your child.
- Stay focused on your child's attributes.
- Involve your child in planning events for fun.

# making home a positive place for learning

Make your home an environment where your dyslexic child feels comfortable and accepted. The goal for every child is to gradually gain independence; the dyslexic child is no different. There are some areas in which your child will always need help. But in others, he will gradually gain mastery, and you will need to step back and allow him to experience his accomplishments on his own.

Help your dyslexic child at home by establishing routines and structure, by making sure that he gets enough rest, and by being available for emotional and practical support. School and the outside world (as you will see in the next chapter) are two places where your child may often encounter the unexpected. Home, however, should be a fairly predictable, safe haven for your dyslexic child.

Home is the place of safety and comfort, and this is particularly important for the child with dyslexia. There is no manual for creating a safe and comfortable home environment, but the basic principles discussed in this chapter will help guide you. For example, establishing dependable routines and providing a comfortable work space and the tools necessary for your child to do his homework are significant ways you can help. Offering your support when your child needs it and encouraging him as he masters steps toward meeting his goals are also essential. A loving, supportive home environment gives your child a solid base from which to grow and learn.

# 17. Strategies for Success in the Outside World

**Most of your young child's time** will be spent in the environment of home or school, but as he grows older, he'll be stepping more frequently into the outside world. For some dyslexic children, learning to navigate the world without a parent at their side may be a frightening experience. However, with your support, confidence, and practical advice, your child will learn to function independently and achieve success.

## advance preparation is the cornerstone

There are many challenges you will be able to prepare your child to meet—as well as unexpected situations that you will not be able to plan for in advance. In this chapter, I'll look at some of the ways you can help your child prepare for both types of experiences as he begins to step outside the home without you.

## "I Can Go Places on My Own"

*Twelve-year-old Tom rides his bike to the grocery store for his mom when she runs out of a particular item. So he won't get lost, he records the directions to the store on a small tape recorder he places in his jacket pocket. When his mom runs out of something she needs, she cuts out the label and gives it to Tom to use as the grocery list. Tom can go to the store with the directions in his pocket and a picture of the item he needs. This is one of his responsibilities as part of the family, and he's proud that he's able to help.*

- Let your dyslexic child know it's okay to ask for help with directions.

- Make use of a tape recorder for directions. Or let your child help make a color-coded map. For instance, using a map of the school, you could draw a line in yellow to indicate the route he follows to classes on Tuesdays; use blue for Wednesday and so on.

- Go on a run-through together before he sets off on his own.

- Use color to help your child remember left and right. A red scrunchie around your daughter's right wrist or a small red dot made on that wrist with a marker could indicate right.

- Teach your child to pay attention to landmarks. For example, turn right at the blue picket fence or left at the fountain.

- Provide your child with a small pad and pencil to carry at all times. Encourage him to ask others to write information down when necessary.

- Use a multisensory approach—auditory, visual, tactile—to directions. For instance, use a tape recorder so your child can hear directions as he's seeing them. Cut out a picture of a landmark from a magazine for reference. Look for more than one way he can absorb information.

- Encourage your child to follow his instincts.

## "I Can Use My Support Team"

*Abe and his best friend have driven to the hockey game. When they park the car, Abe says, "I hope you'll remember where the car is, because I won't have a clue." Dirk, who has just gotten his license, responds, "Don't worry. I have a sixth sense when it comes to directions."*

- Use the buddy system whenever possible.
- Teach your child to ask police officers, teachers, friends, and other responsible individuals for assistance when needed.
- Know what your child can and cannot do. Help him to recognize his weak areas (as well as his strengths) so he will know when he needs to reach out for help.

## "I Can Use Technology"

*Spencer, who is dyslexic, is meeting his friend at the roller-skating rink. The two 13-year-old boys live on opposite ends of town, but each has part of a walkie-talkie set. They check in with each other as they approach the rink. Jack thinks it's a cool game, but for Spencer the walkie-talkies are more—they are his safety net to find his way around town.*

- Provide your child with a walkie-talkie set that he can use with friends.
- If you can afford it, consider giving your child a cell phone. (You might look into family plans, which allow you two or more phones for one monthly fee.)
- Keep abreast of new developments in technology that may be of use to your child, such as voice-activated programs for the computer.

## "I Can Get Organized for Success"

*Ellen, a 14-year-old aspiring artist, has an 8:30 A.M. painting class on Saturdays. She loves to paint, but it's difficult for her to make it to the class on time. She sets her alarm and leaves herself an extra half-hour for preparation. The night before, she packs her sketch pad and other materials so that she won't have to search for them in the morning.*

- Don't expect your dyslexic child to "wing it." Allow extra time for preparation.
- When she's visiting a new place or embarking on a new adventure, make sure your child is not rushed.
- Provide her with a digital wristwatch.

## "Repetition Helps Me Remember"

*Ivy has trouble remembering names. Her mom knows she's often embarrassed because she easily forgets even the names of her classmates. When a new girl moves in next door, Ivy's mom makes a point of using her name often until Ivy remembers it. After several months, Ivy feels confident greeting Margo by name.*

- Use repetition to help your child remember names and other pieces of information.
- Repeat directions in a clear, concise manner.
- To help learn names and other facts, have your child repeat the words and write them down.

## "I Need Help with Telling and Tracking Time"

*Ken knows it's time to go to religion class because* Wheel of Fortune *has just come on TV. He's not great at telling time, and sometimes he has difficulty reading the numbers, but he's figured out ways to help him keep track of his schedule.*

- Help your child learn to tell time; don't rely on school alone to teach this concept. He will need reinforcement at home.
- Provide digital clocks as well as analog clocks.

Routines are part of life. We all have expectations of what will happen during the day, so when someone throws a monkey wrench into our plans, we have to readjust our thinking. Dyslexic kids do best when they have routines to follow, yet it's important to give them coping strategies for those unexpected changes and events that can always crop up.

Morning routines are especially important for dyslexic individuals. If a dyslexic child forgets to brush her teeth or comb her hair, she may feel off-center for the rest of the day. Picture charts are great for helping young kids through morning routines. Another good strategy, which often works well for older kids, is to make up a checklist and have your child cross off the steps as he completes them. This method also works well for packing backpacks. I use this method at work when I hire a new employee. I have about 50 steps I must take to train and prepare the new person; the only way I can make sure I've covered all the bases is to keep a running checklist. Providing your child with a checklist he can follow on his own helps boost his feelings of independence and capability. You will need to help out at the beginning, but in time, he'll be able to follow the list on his own.

Here is an example of a child's morning routine. You can make a chart like this with your child. Provide a place to hang it and a marker to check off the steps.

- Teach your child to observe other clues to time. For instance, when his favorite TV show ends, it's 8:00 P.M. and time to take a bath. Try other clues as well, such as a grandfather clock that chimes on the hour.

- Help your child estimate how long it will take to complete a task.

*Hannah's Morning Schedule*

7:00   Alarm rings. Get out of bed!

7:05   Use bathroom, take shower. Comb hair.

7:15   Get dressed.

7:25   Eat breakfast.

7:45   Feed cat.

7:50   Wash hands and brush teeth.

8:00   Get coat and backpack, and out the door!

Here's an example of a backpack checklist. You can use color-coded checklists to differentiate the backpack contents needed for different days of the week. For example, Monday's red list will include the science and music book. Tuesday's green list will include gym shorts and the vocabulary book.

*Ernie's Backpack/Tuesday/Thursday Schedule*
- Lunch bag
- Gym shorts
- Vocabulary book
- Math book
- Homework file
- Reading book
- Miscellaneous projects

- Encourage him to arrive early and get organized before an event or meeting.

- Encourage your child to check his appointment book or daily planner for the next day's schedule before he goes to sleep at night.

- Use self-adhesive notes to remind your child of appointments.

## Time Issues

Time can be a tricky issue for a dyslexic child. In fact, the multidimensional aspects of time can be complicated for any child at first.

I find that I do much better with a digital clock, but my son, Kevin, who is not dyslexic, says that I'm losing the "perspective" of time when I refuse to use an analog clock. Kevin uses the movement of the hands of the clock to give him a sense of the length and breadth of time; he can look at the long hand inching toward the halfway mark and get a feel for the amount of time that makes up half an hour. I find this to be confusing.

Sometimes I look at an analog clock and can't tell what the hands mean. Is the small hand headed toward the nine, or is it still on the eight? Is it before or after nine o'clock? Many people with dyslexia are confused by such time concepts. If your child is like me, he may benefit from a digital clock. Occasionally, you may want to set a timer or an alarm to help him know when it's time to stop or start an activity.

## "I Can Use Visual Clues"

*Courtney has trouble reading directions, but she can follow a diagram. Her mother reads the complex directions for putting together the new futon bed she had bought for Courtney's room but still seems confused. Courtney looks at the diagrams that accompany the brochure text and puts the futon bed together in record time. Her mom is really impressed.*

- Help your child recognize and use visual clues. Practice frequently.

- Use self-adhesive notes, wall charts, and so on to help your child understand information.

## "I Can Learn to Be More Social"

*Ray, 13, doesn't read social clues very well; he may intrude on others' personal space without meaning to. His mom notices that Ray stands too close when talking to people. She has to remind him about standing back when speaking to a friend.*

- Help your child prepare for social situations. Use role playing to practice appropriate responses that can be used in social settings.

### Role Playing

An effective method for teaching social skills that I often use in my practice is role playing. You can also use role playing at home to help your child hone or master her social skills. For instance, if your daughter is uncomfortable making play dates with other kids or joining in board games at the recreation center, you can practice dialogue with her at home. Pretend that you are a child with a game. Ask your daughter what she would say first. You may need to prompt your child to make sure she gives an appropriate response. The conversation might go like this.

Mom: "Hi." ("What would you say if you wanted to join in?")
Daughter: "Hi. Can I play?"
Mom: "Sure. Which game do you want to play first?"
Daughter: "How about Monopoly?"
Mom: "Okay. That sounds like fun."
(pretending game is over)
Mom: "I won!" ("What would you say to make me feel good?")
Daughter: "That's great. Congratulations!"
Mom: "Thanks." ("What would you say if you wanted to play again?")
Daughter: "Do you want to play again, or would you like to play Sorry now?"

- Talk about and help your child become aware of body language, personal space, and the pitch and volume of his speaking voice.
- Seek outside professional help if social challenges become a major problem. A therapist or social worker can help with teaching your child social skills.

## "I Need Practice Using Money"

*At the swim club, 11-year-old Jerry comes back from the snack bar with 25 cents. His mom asks him where the other dollar is. Jerry seems mystified; he didn't even think about how much money the clerk should have given him.*

- Counting change may be a problem for the dyslexic child. Help your child figure out how much money he will get back in change.
- Practice counting money at home.
- Come as close to exact change as possible when giving your child money to spend.
- Monopoly, or even Junior Monopoly, may be a good game to practice using money skills. Remember, however, that board games involving knowledge of trivia or memory will probably not be enjoyable for your dyslexic child.

## "Help Me Find Places to Succeed"

*Ten-year-old Roger loves sports, but his baseball coach insists on explaining everything in lengthy detail. So when Roger steps up to the plate, he can't even remember the first thing his coach said. When Roger's dad notices that his son's interest in the sport is flagging, he decides to have a talk with the coach. He explains that Roger learns best kinesthetically (that is, with movement) and asks the coach to show rather than tell him the moves.*

- Help your child find a nonacademic extracurricular sport or activity (music, art, or other area) that he will enjoy.
- Pay close attention to the coaching or teaching methods used.
- Talk to the instructor and explain how your child learns best.
- If the instructor is not amenable, try to find one who is.
- Make sure the instructor uses methods that bolster your child's self-esteem.

# let him learn to take charge

It's important for your dyslexic child to know that she is in charge of her life. Although she can and should ask others for help, there are also many things she can do on her own to ensure her success in the outside world. Planning ahead, giving herself plenty of time to accomplish tasks, and taking advantage of advances in technology are just a few of the methods she can use to master her own environment.

Another tip I encourage dyslexic children to use is to "go to their best modality." This means that, whenever possible, your child should use her best method of learning or expressing herself, whether that method is visual, auditory, or tactile. Since I have trouble reading and writing, for instance, I often respond to e-mails by calling the person on the phone or seeking him out in person. I do much better expressing myself verbally than I do writing a note or letter. If your child learns best by listening, she can use a tape recorder to gather information, or she can try talking about a subject with a knowledgeable friend rather than reading a book about it. This is a great technique your child can use.

One of the most important questions during the teen years is "Who am I?" For a teenager with dyslexia, this question is exacerbated because of the problems associated with the disability. Instead of worrying just about who she is, the dyslexic teen must also wonder, "What am I capable of doing?" Self-esteem is also a compelling issue. All teens grapple with this, but the questions may be intensified in the dyslexic adolescent.

Every teen is on the threshold to adulthood, asking the question, "Who will I be?" Your dyslexic teen is wondering if whether who she wants to be will be hindered by her learning differences. Will she be able to be a writer? Will she be able to work in a job that requires a lot of reading? Will she be able to work in a profession that requires a precise knowledge of numbers or that involves the ability to follow complicated directions? Along with the hormonal and developmental issues that all teens face, your dyslexic teen is grappling with added uncertainties.

In junior high and high school, academics become more competitive. Choosing and being accepted to a college becomes an issue, and homework and testing escalate. As a parent, you are not as involved with your child on a daily basis as you were when he was younger. But on an emo-

It's also important for your dyslexic child to know that often she can "buy time" until she is ready. Although there will be occasions when an immediate response is needed, there are also plenty of times when she can say, "I'll get back to you on that" or "I need to think about that; I'll give you a call tomorrow." Let her know that she can determine whether she needs to give an immediate response or

tional basis, you are every bit as important. It's essential for parents to know that they are crucial supporters in their teen's life. By high school, it is absolutely essential that the dyslexic teen has all his support systems in place. Friends, family, teachers, coaches, advisors, and scout or religious leaders all have an important role in guiding the teen. When the going gets rough (as it is bound to), these are the people who will pull your teen through. That is why facing the problems of dyslexia and developing solid support systems early on are absolutely essential.

Teens with dyslexia who have not developed support systems or who have not been properly diagnosed may turn to drugs or alcohol to relieve their stress. Feelings of frustration and anxiety can mount. To complicate matters, teens want desperately to fit in. The tutor who helped your teen may suddenly seem "uncool" and mark her as being "different." During these years, teens may rebel against the very support systems they need so much. Try to be firm yet loving during these potentially difficult years. Keep in mind that you and your teen will get through this period and that the future for your dyslexic adolescent can be as bright as any other child's.

whether she can take some time. Talk about examples that illustrate this idea.

Although you are the parent, ultimately your child is in charge of her own life. With the proper support and tools, your dyslexic child will find ways to work independently and well in the world beyond home and school.

a bright future

# part 5

# 18. Beyond the School Years

**The strategies and concepts** presented in this book will help your child as he navigates his school years with dyslexia, but as I noted earlier, this is a condition that remains into adulthood. Your child will need to continually seek ways to manage the challenges of dyslexia as he grows older. Many of the techniques that work for your child now will be effective through the years. For instance, I still use a support team, and I still follow a daily routine to help me manage my dyslexia.

To help you picture your child's future, let's take a look at how an average day in my life goes and how dyslexia plays a part in how I deal, as an adult, with the ordinary problems and obstacles that fall in my path.

## a day in the life

On an ordinary day, I get up at around 5:00 A.M. Keep in mind that I go to bed early, too! My brain just works better that way, and I know it, so I try to maintain the pattern whenever possible. Part of my success in dealing with dyslexia has to do with my keen awareness of the most efficient ways I think and work. As I've pointed out, you can encourage your child to pay attention to his instincts and to his own knowledge about how his body and mind work best.

## Early Morning

Early in the morning, I pour myself a cup of coffee and head to my computer. I check my e-mail and usually encounter my first problem of the day. So, I'm up for only 10 minutes before being acutely reminded that I'm dyslexic! Often, I don't have a problem reading the e-mail—but if a response is required, I may run into trouble. Once in a while, there will be a note from a reporter asking me to e-mail back the answers to five simple questions or something like that. Not knowing of my dyslexia, the reporter probably assumes this might take me all of 10 minutes. But in reality, such a task might take me several hours.

Occasionally, there will be a cryptic note from a colleague or fellow school board member who likes to write long missives using lots of metaphors and analogies. Since I can't make much sense of this, I just skim over those messages.

I respond to the reporter by suggesting she call me later in the day so we can talk. Some people are annoyed by this, I know. They can't figure out why I can't just shoot them back an e-mail, which would be easier for them (and cheaper, no doubt!). However, I have to "go to my best modality," which is speaking rather than writing.

I am able to write a note back to my cowriter on this book, as well, so I know I'm having a pretty good day. On a bad day, my spelling will be horrendous and my thoughts so incohesive there's no point in trying to get them down on paper. I see a couple of mistakes in the e-mail I send her (but obviously, she knows I'm dyslexic so she won't mind!), and the computer automatically corrects a few more (such as the word "and," which I always type "adn"). On the whole, I'm feeling pretty good today. But there are days when I look at my e-mails and am unable to process them all. It's at times like that when I recall how I felt in sixth grade when my teacher told me I was lazy and dumb. But I've learned to pick myself up and move on. There's no time to feel sorry for myself when I have so many responsibilities in my family and career.

## On to the Paper

Once I'm done with my e-mails, I head to the kitchen to look over the newspaper. I don't say "read" the newspaper, because that's not exactly what I do. I look at the pictures and glance at the headlines. If I find an article that seems interesting, I'll try to read it. Most of the time, I don't finish the article or I keep reading but get lost somewhere in the middle. I continue skimming the headlines and eventually go to shower and get dressed. I follow the same routine just about every day.

## Getting the Kids Ready for School

My children, A.J. and Kevin, are old enough now at 13 and 14 to pretty much fend for themselves in the morning. In the old days, when I was a stay-at-home dad, I had to fix breakfast for them. That was fine as long as it didn't involve measuring ingredients, which can be a problem. Today, since my wife, Linda, is away on a business trip and won't be home until later this afternoon, I do have to make sure A.J. takes her medicine for an ear infection. The two of us take great pains to make sure she gets the right amount, reading the directions several times very carefully.

A.J. needs a note for her teacher, explaining in detail why she missed a deadline for a paper. The reason has to do with the ear infection and the trip we had to make to the doctor, but it's much too complicated for me to put down on paper. I promise A.J. I will call her teacher at school as soon as I get to work. Writing a note in such a hurry about a topic as seemingly simple as this is just too complicated for me.

## Getting to Work

I drop A.J. and Kevin at school and proceed to my office. I follow the same route every day, so there isn't a problem here. In my office, I call A.J.'s teacher and leave a voice-mail message. Then I sit down at my computer and encounter the e-mail problem again. If I need to write someone back in a hurry, I will first e-mail the draft to my wife in her office and wait for her to edit it and send it back to me. Since she's out of town today, however, it's fortunate that I don't have to respond immediately to any messages.

I check my phone messages, too, hoping that no one needs a school brochure. But sure enough, there's a student with a lengthy name who wants one mailed to her. I'll get my secretary to do that. There's also a phone call from a professor in another department whose name is unfamiliar. I'll have to call over there and say, "This is Dr. Frank, returning your call." Hopefully, the right person will pick up on the other end. If not, I'll say, "Someone from your department called here. But the name was cut off. It sounded something like . . . ," and hope I'll eventually be passed on to the correct individual.

Just my luck, the dean drops by as I'm hanging up the phone. He says he forgot to tell me he needs that update report on curriculum by this afternoon. I tell him I'll be happy to get it to him by tomorrow. I have the report nearly finished at home, but there's no way I can rush an important document through on such short notice.

As soon as he leaves, I get out my notes for today's classes and go over them carefully. Even though I have taught many of these classes for 10 or more years, it helps me to refresh my memory before going into the classroom.

## On to Class

At 9:00, 10:00, and 11:00 A.M., I teach my classes. Though I used to avoid it, I've been writing on the board more often, and occasionally, I'll draw a diagram or chart. Most of the time, however, I use prepared overheads, which the students can easily see and comprehend. Once in a while, I'll forget a word when I'm teaching, and I'll call on my students for assistance (they're part of my support team, just as I'm part of theirs). They love to pitch in with the answer, especially some of my nursing/anatomy majors, who are great with medical terms that sometimes pop up in my developmental psychology classes.

Today, I'm assigning a paper that will be due in 2 weeks. I'll have about 50 of these that I'll have to read and correct. I provide the students with very specific instructions on how I want the paper organized. This is a learning experience for them, and it helps me when it comes time to correct the papers (it's also a method that many nondyslexic teachers use). Since I'll have 50 papers with five sections in each, I'll know exactly what I'm looking for in each section.

My students know I'm dyslexic, so if I forget a word here or there, they call out to help. Because I love teaching and put so much preparation into it, I'm usually at peak performance in the classroom, and thankfully, my students are very supportive.

## Interview Time

After a brief lunch and a half-hour tutoring session with a student, I head to the committee room where I'm scheduled to interview two candidates for a teaching position. The last time I led one of these meetings, it was morning, and I brought along about $10 worth of sweet rolls. I mention this only because I never did get reimbursed for that expenditure; it seemed like too much trouble to fill out the form, which doesn't have any lines on it and must be completed in longhand. For a dyslexic individual, this can be a time-consuming and irritating process! I opted instead to take the $10 out of my own pocket.

Although the two interview sessions go well and I have other faculty members there to provide input, I can feel that my concentration level is beginning to wane as the day wears on. Fortunately, my role is to ask questions, not to write down answers, and I'm able to conduct the interviews with relative ease. By 4:30, when I head over to watch A.J.'s basketball game, I'm pretty exhausted. The level of concentration required to get through this day has been very taxing. Normally, I wouldn't have scheduled two interviews on a day when I also had a heavy morning teaching load, but due to extenuating circumstances, it had to be that way.

## Evening at Last

Linda is back, so we prepare dinner together and sit down with the kids to eat and chat. Tonight, they do most of the talking because I'm so worn out from my day. Fortunately, A.J. and Kevin don't need much help with their homework. Kevin, who is academically gifted, rarely needs assistance, and he's usually more than happy to give A.J. help when she needs it.

After helping clean up the kitchen, I retreat to the den, turn on the TV, and watch some sports before bed. I really enjoy watching sports, but often I can't remember the score. Isn't it great that they superimpose the score in the corner of the screen every few minutes? After a day like today, chances are I won't even remember which teams are playing! This can lead to some pretty funny conversations at the watercooler in the morning, when a colleague asks, "Say, did you see that great game last night?" and I answer, "I sure did! Who won?"

Linda, meanwhile, is editing a couple of student recommendations I've written. She rarely if ever complains about helping me out; we each pitch in to the family in different ways. The kids are very supportive, too. They'll correct me if I get a word wrong, and sometimes we'll all laugh about it. My mom, in Arizona, helps when she can, too. If I can't reach Linda during the day, I may give Mom a call and read her a passage over the phone. It's risky, but better than sending the work out without having it reviewed.

By 9:00, Linda and I have a brief chat about our day, tuck in the kids, and hit the sack. Tomorrow, I'll get up extra early to finish up that report for the dean.

# bad days

The day I just described was a good but busy day. Had it been a bad day for me, I would have had greater difficulty getting through the tasks at hand. As it was, by the time I got home from school, my thoughts were sluggish. I would not have been able to write anything down or remember certain simple facts.

Some days, the concentration it takes to manage my dyslexia makes me feel emotionally drained, but I use my strategies, and I can usually get by. As an adult, I can handle my setbacks better than I could when I was a child. I know that I may need more time to think about an issue or that I may have to wait until the next day to resolve a problem, but I'm confident that I will eventually arrive at the answer.

As an adult with a thorough understanding of dyslexia, I no longer fear that I am dumb or stupid as I did as a child. And I'm not afraid to tell people about my condition (though sometimes I may choose not to) or to ask for help when I need it. As an adult, I have more patience with myself. I don't become angry or frustrated when I can't respond to a question immediately or when I misspell or mispronounce a word. I have come to accept that there are certain words I will probably never spell right.

## great strides

Each day in my life as an adult, I encounter difficult situations in which I must read, spell, recall a fact, follow a direction, or complete some other task that is hindered by my dyslexia. But although reading, writing, and spelling are a big part of life, they're not *all* of life, and I have put these things into perspective. Of course, I wish I could read the newspaper from front to back or write a paragraph without needing to have it edited, but I know that's not going to happen. When I walk down the hall at school, my students and colleagues don't look at me and think, "Here comes Dr. Frank. He's dyslexic." They simply see their teacher or friend and wave or smile. Because I accept myself, know what I can and can't do, utilize my strengths whenever possible, and seek ways to work with my weaknesses, my dyslexia has not held me back from my goals.

With help from family, friends, and others, your child, too, will make great strides. Dyslexia complicates the process, but it also inspires honesty, determination, and optimism that truly enhance life.

# 19. As Life Goes On

As life goes on, your child will live and learn with dyslexia. The strategies presented in this book, coupled with your love and support, will help him to reach many of his goals. Make no mistake about it: You can make a difference in your dyslexic child's life. I'd like to share with you a few comments I've received from some dyslexic students and adults. Perhaps these will help you understand the secret life of the dyslexic child even more profoundly.

## looking at others

I often ask the dyslexic individuals I meet how dyslexia has changed or affected their lives. Invariably, I get the response that it has made them stronger, better people. As I remarked in chapter 10, I do not view dyslexia as a "gift." However, I do know that in many ways, dyslexia inspires people to draw upon their inner strengths in a positive manner. Dyslexia also naturally makes people look at themselves more closely than they might ordinarily do, in order to examine their strengths and weaknesses.

## From Benjamin, a 17-Year-Old College Student

"I freak out right before I take tests. My mind just freezes. I look over the material right before the test so it is nice and clear in my head. But when that test is put right in front of me, I just lose it. Then I try to speed through the test while the answers are still clear in my mind's eye, so I can hurry up and try to put down the right answers. Then when I do that, I misread the questions because I read them too fast. I still get them wrong. I don't know why this has to be an issue for me.

"When I was taking the test with Dr. Frank, I felt comfortable. I don't feel comfortable or trust many people. I feel that teachers will judge me and think differently of me if I don't know the answers. I don't want them to think that I'm dumb or stupid. That is why I never really seek help.

"I have always had an issue with self-esteem, although I think that I have gotten better. Actually, I know that I have. I think a lot of the whole self-esteem issue had to do with school. Of course, here and there occasionally, I would get made fun of by my peers. I guess I probably figured if my peers were going to judge me, then my teachers would do the same. I guess I didn't know any better. I think I would do better if I were on more of a one-on-one basis with teachers.

"Testing in high school was hard. Because I didn't do well in high school, I just didn't care. The career counselor told me that no college would accept me because of my grades. She told me that there was no point in my taking the ACT tests. She said that the only chance I had was to attend a community college. She said that if I did well at community college, then there was a chance that someday I could transfer to a university or a different college. So I am trying my hardest to do well. So far, I think I have succeeded. I'm a B-average student now. I never thought that I could do well in school. So far, in community college, not one teacher has approached me about my test-taking. No teacher has asked me what my problem is.

"In grade school, I always knew there was something wrong with me. I had problems comprehending what I read in class. But still to this day, I do find it hard to concentrate at times. However, I know that I'm not dumb. I always thought that I was at times. But I know that I'm not. It just takes me longer than other people to finally understand a concept or anything in general. I accept that. I accept that, and I'm fine with it. It still doesn't make me a bad person or stupid."

## From Mike, a Dyslexic Adult

"The main thing is recognizing dyslexia and dealing with it emotionally. I have developed a series of defenses and a sense of humor. Even at my age—62—I still get very angry at myself if I transpose an important phone number or if I write something by hand in final form, such as a greeting card, and leave out or misspell a word. My wife, Rochelle, helps by proofing everything. I have trouble reading. As Fern, my mom, would say, I do not decode or process the words correctly. As a defense mechanism, I read slowly. The major problem is that I do not always see small words such as 'no' or 'not.' Needless to say, this changes the meaning of the sentence. But because I read to understand, my brain will tell me, 'Hey, the last sentence doesn't make sense with the previous content!' Then I read it again.

"I will reverse numbers when writing them down or repeating them. I can do math, including percentages, in my head without any problem. Having a spouse who understands and assists is a major benefit. Never does she make fun or ridicule, but she and I often laugh together when I tell her how I screwed up or misread a sentence.

"When I worked as a customs agent and had cases involving an automobile, I would often ask my partner to get the license plate number, and I would get the make and model of the car.

"Even today, if someone gives me a phone number, I will read it back to make sure I have it right. Another trick I use: When someone gives me a phone number, I write it in larger-than-normal numbers. I find larger writing helps to prevent the reversal for some reason.

"I never knew what was wrong, other than that I had trouble in school, including college. When I dated Rochelle in our last year of college and she was getting her degree in special ed, one night she called me and told me she had just read in a textbook all about me. That night was the first time anyone ever told me what I had."

## From Margie, Mother of Two Dyslexic Children

"My kids actually get lost on their way to class if their schedule changes. If, for instance, there's an assembly at school and the day starts with period four, my boys have to walk the path to periods one, two, and three before they can end up in the right room for period four. They have terrible problems with their locker combinations, so they carry around 30-pound book bags all day. It's hard enough for them to know which classrooms to go to. They can't handle stopping at the locker and knowing that they won't be able to get that locker open on the first or second try. Many times, they gave up and left their lockers open and had their belongings taken. Now, they just cart everything with them all day long.

"My advice is: Be an advocate for your child. It's imperative that you figure out how to ask questions in a way that does not intimidate your child's teachers or put them off, and you must figure out how to get the teachers to be on your child's side.

"But the most important advice I can give to parents is to find out what it's like for your child, to look deep inside and understand his secret life."

# a final message

I hope that you, as a parent, now realize that dyslexia will always be a reality and a challenge for your child in his daily life. But just as importantly, I want you to realize that dyslexia can be managed and that *with your help*, your child will meet his goals and achieve his dreams.

As you proceed on the adventure of helping your child grow to become a happy, successful adult, I hope you'll keep the following points in mind. They have surely helped me as I've struggled with dyslexia throughout my life, and I know that they will be useful to your child as well.

## For Your Child

Make sure your child learns to keep these points in mind.

**"Use your best modality."** Remind your child to go to his best method of learning or communicating whenever possible.

**"Don't be afraid to ask for help."** Let him know it's okay to get help from others and to build a strong support network.

**"Know what you can and cannot do."** Help your child to be realistic about his strengths and weaknesses.

**"Be honest about your dyslexia."** Encourage your child to let others know about how his disability affects his life and his learning style.

**"Trust your instincts."** Help your child learn to listen to his body's rhythms and messages.

**"Be patient with yourself."** Let your child know it is okay to ask for more time if he needs it.

## For Parents and Educators

**Know that you can make a difference.** Your support can make a crucial difference in your dyslexic child's life at home, school, and in the outside world.

**Adjust, but don't lower your expectations.** Help your child set realistic goals and dreams.

**Focus on his abilities, not his disabilities.** Help your child find places where he can excel and have fun.

**Be an advocate.** You are your child's best supporter. Never give up seeking ways to help him learn and achieve.

**Believe in your child.** Your support means everything.

**Enjoy your child.** Remember to cherish and appreciate your child every day.

# the road ahead

Many books about learning disabilities like dyslexia make a point of mentioning movie stars or famous athletes with the disability who have achieved their dreams. In this book, I've purposely downplayed this topic, even though there are many such individuals who have achieved great fame and fortune.

Though most parents have high hopes and aspirations for their children, I would venture to guess that most of us don't really envision our kids on movie screens or in the Oval Office (which isn't to say it can't be done—several presidents are reputed to have been dyslexic). What we do want most for our children, however, is for them to be happy and to feel content with the choices they make in life.

I won't go so far as to say that your dyslexic child will never become rich or famous; indeed, she may do just that. But I hope I have led you to understand that your child is capable of making her own decisions, of setting her own goals, and with your help, of finding ways to manage her dyslexia so that she can pursue her interests and aspirations, whatever they may be. Dyslexia is not easy to live with, but neither is it an insurmountable disability. It's my belief, however, that what happens in childhood—and how strongly and deeply a child senses the care and support of her family and others—is what makes the lasting, essential difference in how dyslexia impacts the course of life.

I wish you and your child every success, but most of all, I wish that you and your child will experience the tremendous joy life has to offer—made all the more precious by the concentration and hard work that is involved in living with dyslexia each and every day.

# Resources

## Books

Huston, Anne Marshall. *Understanding Dyslexia: A Practical Approach for Parents and Teachers* (Madison Books, 1992). This well-written, in-depth work is designed for parents and teachers who want to learn more about dyslexia. Much more than a primer, the book is very comprehensive, offering extensive information on the subject and practical strategies for dyslexics.

Jordan, Dale R. *Overcoming Dyslexia in Children, Adolescents, and Adults* (Pro Ed, 1996). I like this book and refer to it often because it translates specialized clinical data into everyday language. It is useful for anyone who needs more practical knowledge on dyslexia.

## Organizations

**All Kinds of Minds**
PO Box 3580
Chapel Hill, NC 27515

Phone: (919) 933-9378

www.allkindsofminds.org

All Kinds of Minds is a private non-profit organization that helps families, educators, and clinicians understand why children are struggling in school and provides practical strategies and programs to help children become more successful learners. All Kinds of Minds was established to continue the pioneering work of Dr. Mel Levine, director of the Clinical Center for the Study of Development and Learning at the University of North Carolina Medical School in Chapel Hill and author of the best-selling *A Mind at a Time*.

### American Speech-Language-Hearing Association (ASHA)

10801 Rockville Pike

Rockville, MD 20852

Phone: (800) 638-8255

www.asha.org

ASHA is a government organization that addresses speech, language, and hearing issues.

### Association on Higher Education and Disability (AHEAD)

University of Massachusetts Boston

100 Morrissey Blvd.

Boston, MA 02125-3393

Phone: (617) 287-3880

www.ahead.org

AHEAD, formerly the Association on Handicapped Student Service Programs in Postsecondary Education, is an international organization committed to full participation in higher education for persons with disabilities.

### Council for Exceptional Children (CEC), Division of Learning Disabilities (DLD)

www.dldcec.org

The CEC is the largest professional organization representing those dedicated to improving educational outcomes for children and youth who are gifted or have disabilities. The DLD is a division of CEC that focuses on learning disabilities.

**Council for Learning Disabilities (CLD)**
PO Box 40303
Overland Park, KS 66204
Phone: (913) 492-8755
www.cldinternational.org

CLD is an international organization of and for professionals who represent diverse disciplines and who are committed to enhancing the educational development of individuals with learning disabilities.

**Educational Resources Information Center (ERIC)**
www.eric.ed.gov

This federally funded, nationwide information network provides access to education literature. ERIC is a program of the U.S. Department of Education and is administered by the National Library of Education.

**The Hello Friend/Ennis William Cosby Foundation**
PO Box 4061
Santa Monica, CA 90411
www.hellofriend.org

The Hello Friend/Ennis William Cosby Foundation was established to celebrate the life and fulfill the goals and dreams of Ennis William Cosby. Ennis's common greeting, "Hello Friend," inspired the name of the Foundation. The foundation was formed in early 1997 as a public, nonprofit organization that promotes early recognition, compassionate understanding, and effective education for individuals with learning disabilities.

**The International Dyslexia Association, International Office (IDA)**
8600 LaSalle Road
Chester Building, Suite 382
Baltimore, MD 21286-2044
Messages: (800) ABCD123
Voice: (410) 296-0232
www.interdys.org

The International Dyslexia Association is an international, non-profit organization dedicated to the study and treatment of dyslexia and maintains a strong presence in educational and scientific communities. The IDA was established to continue the pioneering work of Dr. Samuel T. Orton, a neurologist who was one of the first to begin to identify dyslexia and develop effective teaching approaches.

**Learning Disabilities Association of America (LDA)**
4156 Library Road
Pittsburgh, PA 15234
Phone: (412) 341-1515
www.ldanatl.org

The LDA is a national volunteer organization advocating for individuals with learning disabilities.

**National Center for Learning Disabilities (NCLD)**
381 Park Avenue South, Suite 1401
New York, NY 10016
Phone: (212) 545-7510
www.ncld.org

The NCLD is a national organization providing services and programs for learning-disabled children and adults, their families, teachers, and other professionals.

**National Information Center for Children and Youth with Disabilities (NICHCY)**
PO Box 1492
Washington, DC 20013
Phone: (800) 695-0285
www.nichcy.org
NICHCY provides information and referral on disability-related issues.

**National Institute of Child Health and Human Development (NICHD)**
Building 31, Room 2A32, MSC 2425
31 Center Drive
Bethesda, MD 20892-2425
Phone: (800) 370-2943
www.nichd.nih.gov
NICHD is a part of the National Institutes of Health and has been conducting research on learning disabilities and related disorders. Within the past 10 years, NICHD research has identified the major cognitive mechanisms underlying dyslexia and other learning disabilities and studied how the assessment of these mechanisms can help to predict the onset, developmental course, and outcomes of such disorders.

**Recording for the Blind and Dyslexic (RFB&D)**
20 Roszel Road
Princeton, NJ 08540
Phone: (800) 221-4792
www.rfbd.org
RFB&D is a nonprofit educational library for people who can't read standard print because of a visual, learning, or other physical disability. Founded in 1948, the organization is the first and largest provider of

recorded educational materials to students from kindergarten through post-graduate school who are learning through listening.

**The Schwab Foundation for Learning**
www.schwablearning.org
The Schwab Foundation for Learning offers a wide range of services for parents and educators to provide information, support, and technological tools to improve the lives of students with learning differences.

## Web sites
**www.interdys.org**
This is a very user-friendly site from the International Dyslexia Association (IDA), which has gathered information from many sources to help site visitors understand the causes and effects of dyslexia and methods for testing and treating it.

**www.bda-dyslexia.org.uk**
This site calls itself "the voice of dyslexic people," offering advice, information, and help to families, professionals, and dyslexic individuals and working to raise awareness and understanding of dyslexia.

**www.booksontape.com**
This Web site offers books on tape.

**www.childdreams.com.au/disorder/dyslexia.html**
This Web site provides an overview of the current understanding of dyslexia, including medical and neurological causes, diagnosis, the treatment and management of dyslexia, as well as what dyslexic students may expect for their future.

## www.dyslexia-inst.org.uk

The Dyslexia Institute (DI), an educational charity founded in 1972 for the assessment and teaching of people with dyslexia and for the training of teachers, created this Web site. DI has grown to become the only national dyslexia teaching organization in the world.

## www.dyslexia.net

This Web site was created by the Michigan Dyslexia Institute (MDI), a nonprofit organization serving children and adults with dyslexia. MDI's mission statement is to "envision a new world for children and adults with dyslexia," in which those who have dyslexia feel good about themselves, look forward to the future with hope and confidence, receive the kind of instruction they need in a nurturing environment, and are encouraged to develop their potential in order to participate fully in the workplace and in their communities.

## www.kidshealth.org/teen/school_jobs/school/dyslexia.html

Geared for teens who are dyslexic, this Web site features articles and resources to help them gain a more comprehensive understanding of dyslexia.

## www.playback.net/vision/dyslexia/people.htm

Visit this Web site for a list of famous people with dyslexia.

## www.rfbd.org

This is the Web site for the organization Recording for the Blind and Dyslexic, the nation's educational library for those with print disabilities.

# Index

Underscored page references indicate boxed text.

# h

# i

# j

Responsibilities, giving child
    manageable, 72–73, 159, 209,
    221–23
Rewards for reaching goals, 135–37
Role playing, 219

# S

SATs, 186–87
School. *See also* College success
        strategies
    guidance department in, 187
    Individualized Education Program
        and
        first steps of, 103–6
        post-meeting tasks and, 106
        purpose of, 102–3
        understanding, 104–5
    parallel worlds in
        awareness of, 37–38
        fitting in, 42–43
        grades, 39–40
        mistakes, 40–41
        reading skills, 38–39
        structure and, 41
    requirements, monitoring, 185–86
    special services department in, 148
    success strategies
        classroom changes, 182–83
        communication, 162–64, 163
        flexibility, 184–85
        following directions, 178–79
        Individualized Education Program
            and, 162
        math, 173–74
        note taking, 176–78
        organizing desk, 179–80, 180
        peers, dealing with, 183
        reading, 164–68, 165, 166–69
        spelling, 171–73, 172
        teacher tactics and, 183–84
        test taking, 174–76, 175
        time and sequence aids, 168–70
        timeliness, 181
        writing, 170–71
    support network, 147–48
    surprises in, confusion caused by,
        41–42
    tutor and, finding good, 196–97

School supplies, stocking up on,
    199–201
Secrecy about dyslexia, avoiding, 69–70
Secret life of dyslexic children,
    understanding, 3–5
Self-adhesive notes as reading aid, 166
Self-esteem
    building, 155–60, 156
    developmental aspect of, 161
    importance of, 154–57
    low, 160–61
Sense of touch as spelling aid, 173
Sequence learning aids, 168–70
Setting goals for success
    attending college, 185
    breaking into small steps and, 132
    child's participation in, 130–31
    Individualized Education Program
        and, 129
    long-term, 131
    organization and, 131–32
    realistic goals and, 130
    short-term, 131
    specific goals and, 129–30
    time frame for, 132–33
Short-term goals, setting, 131
Siblings
    explaining diagnosis to, 141
    handling, 209–10
Skills, parental help in building, 158
Sleep habits, fostering good, 193–95
Sociability, 219–20, 219
Spatial skills challenges, 64–66
Specific goals, setting, 129–30
Speech therapy, 104–5
Spelling aids, 171–73, 172
Spelling box, creating, 172, 172
Spouse, game plan for dyslexic
        children and, 142–43, 144–45
Structure in school, importance of,
    41–42
Success
    in adult years, 234
    in college
        ACTs and, 186–87
        assisting with college applications,
            186
        checking out college programs,
            187–88
        matching child and college, 189–90